Lisa and

From Arthur

The Adventures of
TWO
STUDLEY
LADS

So nice to hear about your new
home in Cromer, and I know that
you will be very happy here

And Rich especially my thanks to
you (fellow enlarged prostate sufferer) for
the beautiful carpentry & rails etc
that was to help Pat, so much, and now
me (slipped disc) later. And in memory of
Pat ps. (80 and 84)

Dedicated to
John William Shakles
1941 – 2020
and
Captain Joseph Butler Peart
1885 – 1963

Front Cover: Shakespeare's Warwickshire Countryside.
Rear Cover top: St Mary's Parish Church, Studley.
Rear Cover middle: Spitfire opposite the Barley Mow, Studley.
Rear Cover bottom: Alcester Co-op Society, Grocery and Drapery Store, Studley.

All of the paintings in this book are by Roger Thomas
and have been processed and titled by Robert Bullock.

Unless otherwise stated all of the photographs included in this book
have appeared in the Studley Historian, the thrice-yearly magazine of the
Studley Local History Group, who have kindly agreed to their inclusion.

The Adventures of

TWO STUDLEY LADS

Growing up in Shakespeare's Warwickshire
during the 1940s, 50s and 60s

Arthur Cooke and Roger Thomas

BREWIN BOOKS

BREWIN BOOKS
19 Enfield Ind. Estate,
Redditch,
Worcestershire,
B97 6BY
www.brewinbooks.com

First published by Brewin Books 2022

A CIP catalogue record for this book is
available from the British Library.

ISBN: 978-1-85858-753-0

Printed and bound in Great Britain
by Halstan & Co. Ltd.

CONTENTS

FOREWORD

By Arthur Daniels, President of Studley Local History Group

IN THEIR introduction to this book, the authors, seemingly unlikely bedfellows, set the scene of their following pages: glimpses of a past which is still within touching distance – just.

The reader, in words and pictures, is transported to a vanishing world, many of whose structures remain, though modified in form; sadly, the characters described do not.

Both long-time ex-pats, Arthur a Studley lad and Roger a near neighbour from Middletown, both in Warwickshire, have maintained close connections with their origins. Each has his own story to tell.

Arthur is a diligent researcher of local history and prolific reporter of his findings. Roger, through the sensitive eye of the observer, and his recording through the medium of paint, is a skilled reporter of the visual, enjoying the practise of his skills since childhood, and passing on his enthusiasm for his art.

With confidence I recommend this book as both a good read and a real joy.

PREAMBLE

By Tony Lever, Chairman of Studley Local History Group

DEAR READER I hope you will enjoy Arthur and Roger's trip down memory lane. In some ways these remind me of my own youth and certainly my wife Jean relates strongly to these reflections as she is very familiar with these locations.

It's written into the constitution of the Studley Local History Group that we should aim to preserve our village history and foster the growth of that knowledge within our community; so, we highly commend it for its aims and achievements.

This volume succeeds in preserving a way of life now more difficult to live within, with rules and regulations restricting activities as well as the internet providing a much less healthy way of life.

Oh, how I would have loved to have spent my youth among the fields, streams and valleys, particularly so within this beautiful Warwickshire countryside environment; unlike my own experiences of city life and industrial communities.

Read, imagine and relive your youthful adventures.

Above all enjoy.

ABOUT THE AUTHOR AND ILLUSTRATOR

Arthur Cooke

I WAS born in November 1941 in war-time Britain. The years 1940/41 had witnessed the worst bombing of the industrial Midlands, and I recall my grandmother, Annie Cooke, telling me that, whilst standing at the rear door of their Castle Road cottage, having earlier heard the drone of German bombers, she could see reflections of the fires in the sky over Coventry!

All my paternal ancestors had lived in Redditch Road. My grandmother, Annie Cooke's (née Blick) family lived opposite the Shakespeare public house, which was the venue of her wedding reception after she married Charles Cooke. She descended from the families of Benjamin and Dinah Blick. Benjamin was born in Studley in 1804, and his ancestors may have been among the earliest needle workers in Studley. Historical records reveal that every family member was engaged in needle making of one form or another![1]

Annie (née Blick) and Charles Cooke.

My grandfather's grandparents, Elisha, and Rebecca (née Horton) Cooke, with whom he lived in the Wapping, Redditch Road, moved into the village in the early 19th century, from the Slough. Elisha was a son of Edward Cooke,

---

1   *Studley Historian*, Issue 10, pp.4-6, 'The Blicks of Studley'.

from Sambourne, both were needlemasters (i.e. they were also employers), and it is possible that in 1910 he might have been the only Studley resident who could fashion a needle from a piece of wire! His daughter, Florence, married William Blick, a descendent of Henry Blick, who also lived in Redditch Road and both families exclusively engaged in needle manufacture. As a child it seemed, I was related to everyone in the village![2]

Lance Corporal Albert Cooke, Royal Artillery, Panda Division (Arthur Cooke Collection).

My father, Albert Cooke, like millions more, was conscripted into the armed services, temporarily losing his job as manager of the Alcester Co-operative Butchery in the High Street. Because of this my mother lost the tenancy of the 3-bedroom flat above the shop, causing her and my brother, Peter to live alternately with my grandparents in Alcester or Studley. Consequently, I was born, not in Studley, but in Bidford-on-Avon as my mother's sister, Ida, who lived there, would care for her afterwards. Shortly afterwards I came to Studley with my godparents, aunt Elsie and uncle Gerald Reed, who took me to St Mary's Parish Church for my christening.

Of course, it was difficult for my grandparents Cooke to have my mother and two children in their two bedroomed cottage, so unsurprisingly a search commenced for a more suitable arrangement! Gran and grandad Cooke lived at 32, in the second terrace on the left-hand side of lower Castle Road, daughters Doris Barker and Elsie Read lived at Nos. 30 and 28 and son Charlie at number 18. Doris had learnt of a recently vacated cottage in Littlewood Green and grandad asked to negotiate a tenancy for my mum.

The owner was Tom Watton[3], a scrap metal merchant who lived in Bromsgrove Road. Tom, although illiterate, was a most successful businessperson, due to his

---

2   *Studley Historian*, Issue 11, pp.4-7, 'The Cookes of Studley'.

3   *Studley Historian*, Issue 16, p.9 and *SH* Issue 24, pp.3-6, 'The Wattons of Studley'.

realising the advantages of transporting scrap metal by rail, as this was much in demand during the war. He bought various properties in the village including the old Jubilee public house and adjoining cottages! This former inn had become redundant with the building of the new Jubilee opposite to where Tommy lived in Bromsgrove Road.

It was here, at the bar, where the negotiations took place. Tommy knew my grandad and his family, and was mindful that son, Albert, "was fighting in the war." But he said that he did not want kids in the cottage, but grandad assured him that we were well behaved. But building works needed to be done, before anyone moved in. He knew that grandad was a builder's labourer working for local firm, Wilkes the Builder, so to get the house he would do that work. Grandad agreed, handed over the rent and Tom gave him the key! This cottage became the second of my four homes, if I count 32 Castle Road, in my 20 years in Studley!

Wherever I lived, I would spend a part of my life at my first house, "me gran's." It was there when my interest in our family history and of the village of Studley began. I would sit on her peg rug in front of the black lead fireplace, where she told me the most wondrous stories and sometimes my cousins, who lived in the road, would join me. I can hear the words now "Can we look at your photograph album gran?" This was brought from the stairs and we would look at every photograph, although we had done this so many times before! Later, grandad began working at 'New Factory' (Arrow Works in Birmingham Road) of the 'Needles' (Needle Industry). This new factory was one of the very few new buildings the Government allowed during the war. Gran did outwork which was called 'spitting,' about which, I will explain later.

Arthur

Roger Thomas

I WAS born in September 1943 in Middletown Lane and you could not wish for a better place to live. Surrounded by fields with no restrictions were The Hills and Hollows/The Old Hollow Oak Tree, which Arthur and others recall, and as mentioned in the *Studley Historian* Magazine by others, as part of their growing up in Studley.

It was the countryside that first inspired me to paint, at the tender age of 10, buying oil paints out of my earnings from doing a paper round before I was 11 years of age.

Although my thoughts and memories are still with Studley, which I still visit from time to time, I am busy running two art groups also holding exhibitions of my paintings in Somerset, where I now live with my wife Dorothy.

The aim of this book is to encourage everyone to enjoy the countryside that surrounds Studley and hopefully to inspire every reader to paint, 'but not for profit,' only to enjoy painting.

My grandparents lived all their married lives at number 73 Redditch Road, the Wapping and had sixteen children. My father Maurice was the youngest son and featured in the *Studley Historian*. Granddad retired from the Needle Industry aged seventy-three having been a works police

Roger, aged 19, painting.

officer there after working 44 years at the Enfield Cycle Company Redditch. In his younger days he walked to work from Studley to Birmingham and is featured in issue 16 of the *Studley Historian* Needle Industry Works Fire Service photograph. I remember going to the Nag's Head for his bottle of beer. My grandmother, a trained nurse, was a midwife in Studley as well as Astwood Bank and had to walk there. I was born in the house now called She-Mol, the third eldest of six children. My father was still in the army for the first years of my life. I remember my mother washing me in the sink, under the cold-water pump from the well as we had no running water or electricity in the lane until about 1950, only gas. In the lane living next door was Betty Austin and her parents. In the field opposite Betty made daisy chains and put them around my neck. My friend Phil Archer lived the other side with his family, before he moved to his grandparent's farm in Sambourne. Neville Gibbs lived further down where his father ran a drapery business from the house. Neville and I cycled to London in 1957, aged fourteen, it frightens me to think about it now.

Roger

INTRODUCTION

THE STORIES told by "me gran" and the countless villagers I knew, as well as having lived in four distinct parts of the village, inspired me to write articles in the *Studley Historian* (SH). This began with encouraging words from a life-long friend, the late John Shakles, to whom this book is dedicated. He persuaded the founding editor of SH, and now President of the Studley Local History Group (SLHG), Arthur Daniels to accept a 'within living memory' article from me. My article, the 'Swimming Pools of Studley', is in Issue 3, and I have been writing articles for the magazine ever since!

In issues 55 and 56 Roger agreed to include his paintings and it really went from there! I only knew of Roger when I called in to see an elder brother of his, David. I was so impressed with his paintings in the SLHG calendar 2020 which, although now out of date, hangs above my bureau where I write. It is coincidental, that we have similar ancestry, as both of our paternal families once lived on the Wapping, Redditch Road. But, whereas Roger's move into agriculture took him further into the countryside my final house moves in Studley made me more of a 'townie'.

The Wapping, Redditch Road (SLHG).

It is difficult to explain, but when I write about Studley, I'm back in the village of my childhood. As for Roger, it was his fondness of the countryside around the village that gave him the love of painting. Roger's creative work was inspired by his employer, farmer Captain Peart and the book is also dedicated to him. We said by e-mail to one another "Why don't we produce a book together, my stories and your paintings?" This is that book.

But it is not simply a collection of those articles and paintings but the story of our early years in post-war Studley! In addition, for the benefit of those who want to know more, the text contains footnotes which will take you to details of source in SH and other publications. I know SLHG are more than happy to print and send earlier issues to you for a small charge. In addition, maps within the covers of this book illustrate the roads and features mentioned.

There are no chapters as such, as this is the unfolding story of our first years in the village and simply the continuing beautifully illustrated story of our memories. It begins with my first memories, and it ends, the day after my late wife, Pat, and I were married, as we moved to a new home near London. We have returned thousands of times but never to reside, but I know that I will re-join Pat in the village we love so well!

We have quite deliberately excluded most photographs of buildings which are still there, but as the village has lost so many, have purposely included photographs and paintings of those which played a role in our early lives.

ADVENTURES

Jubilee Yard, Littlewood Green

MY STORY begins in my second home, the entrance to which was through the arch visible in the photograph below.

Our house was in the middle of the yard at the back of the terraced houses you can see to the left of the old pub and, unlike them, it had only one room downstairs and two bedrooms above. It had just one exterior door and three windows on the side facing the yard and alongside were shared detached flush toilets. These did not have water cisterns so water was drawn from a tap and trough in the yard and carried by bucket to the WC.

Kindly Mrs Watton in the adjacent big house (the former pub) was our matron, and especially helpful to 'war mums', by helping with family crises from bruised knees to swallowed whistles! Her daughter, Mary Brazil wrote in her

The 'old' Jubilee, Littlewood Green, circa 1913 (SLHG).

informative articles on the Watton family and their residences.[4] "There were no houses on the opposite side where the Grove is now and this field was used by Mr Perkins (a hay and straw dealer) who had a small barn in Bromsgrove Road. There was a small barn and haystack which I remember young Peter Cooke falling from and fracturing his jaw; I am sure that it was 'send for Mrs Watton'."

I remember playing in the Wattons' huge garden with their daughter, Ann and being taken by her parents to places, including Dudley Zoo and watching motorbike speedway riders somewhere in Birmingham. We had fascinating visits to Golbourne's farm which was lower down Bromsgrove Road and opposite the junction of Watts Road. Once the farmer squirted milk on me as he milked a cow in the barn! It sounds unhealthy, but on one occasion Peter and I stood as he poured milk into a cooler, afterwards giving each of us a cupful and it was beautiful.

Just around the corner mum might use Feasey's grocery shop, which was then only the area behind the door and window on the left of this photograph. Mum could also get her sewing needs at Annie Craner's shop along the Bromsgrove Road, but if she needed more things, she walked the one mile to either the High Street or Alcester Road. If it were the former, taking her along Crooks Lane near to where the entrance of Studley High School is today, she would pass by Bownes' where on the return journey she might buy potatoes in the shop, which

The shop on the corner of Littlewood Green and Bromsgrove Road (SLHG).

---

4   *Studley Historian*, Issue 16, p.9 and *SH* Issue 24, pp.3-6, 'The Wattons of Studley'.

was little more than Albert and Rose's front room. She would also pass the more modern and larger Frost's shop, which was near the entrance to the 'Rec' (the recreation ground), before reaching the High Street.

In the High Street Duffin's shop was quite large but at grocers Sutor's or nearby greengrocer Draycott's there were queues. Inside Sutor's there was enough room for shopkeeper Edgar or son John behind the counter and about two shoppers, as each purchase was placed one at a time into their bags. It was a cash transaction or 'on the slate' (for a later payment). As mum shopped the shopkeeper would cut out the appropriate coupons from her ration book. These were issued from the outset of war for most items of food and clothing and everyone was given coupons deemed to be sufficient for their needs. The next shop for mum would be Draycott's, where Albert and Dorothy would come around their counter to put vegetables in shopping bags. Then, off to nearby Dyson's wet fish shop and next door was the tiny shop of my great-uncle Harry Westbury, the cobbler, where there was barely enough room for him, yet alone a customer, so mum would just open the door and say, "Hullo."

Mum would rarely go down Fleece Hill (the lower part of the High Street) where on the left there was the larger shop of Mason's grocers. But if there was a long queue at Franklin's, who were waiting for another batch of loaves from their bakers' ovens, she might go down the hill to the tiny shop of Hunt's bakers. She could call at Nellie Hall's haberdashery which was next to Franklin's and sometimes go next door to the Co-op butchers, which being much larger inside, made queueing easier, especially when it was raining. Leaving there we passed by Crow's hardware shop and, if I were lucky, we might call into Mrs Jones's tiny sweetshop with its gas lamp outside, but since most sweets were on ration a dried twig of liquorice plant would suffice.

A journey to Alcester Road necessitated travelling along Toms Town Lane, 'Back' (New) Road, passing a tiny shop just before the Convent and then via Church Street. If there was not a queue we might call into Redfern's, and then into the much larger Co-op grocers but there was always a queue inside. However, the biggest difference between those queues and the ones I witnessed during the 2020/1 'Lockdowns', is that no-one seemed impatient, with everyone communicating the latest family or Studley news.

It took a long time with 'Silv' Canning or Les Gameson wrapping up individual items, cutting off blocks of butter or cheese, pouring sugar into blue bags, slicing ham or bacon and writing a bill. Coupons and cash were taken, put in a metal container and whisked along by overhead wire to Tommy Knight, sitting in a little office above. The money counted, a dividend slip written and the change returned in the container, then to the counter. The building also housed the draper but, since mum made all our clothes, we had no need to go in there. Lower down from there opposite Manor Road was the shop of John and Daisy Bulmer with its tiny window, which I could not reach, but inside there was a long glass topped counter filled with interesting things!

The doctor did not have an appointment system in place, so we sat in the waiting room, in Alcester Road and gradually shuffled round until next to his surgery door where you became 'first in the queue'. Whilst this was happening the patients chatted amongst themselves. If a prescription was issued it was taken to Timothy Whites & Taylors Chemist, further along Alcester Road and there you might be told "come back this afternoon" or "come back tomorrow". Mum might go towards Bell Lane and call at the little grocers' shop of Ambrose and Lizzie Powell or a short walk further to the wool shop of Rose and Harry Rose! If her soldiers' pay and benefits were due, she would call at the 'new post office', run by the Haynes family and then take a rest on one of the facing benches between there and the chemist. Finally, loaded with bags, she would start the long walk home, passing by the 'old post office' (Johnson's hardware and newspaper

The "Old Post Office" and other shops in Alcester Road and on the left Thompson's Brewery with the Needle Industries Central Works in the background, by Roger Thomas.

shop), past Foster's hardware shop, having crossed the road into New Road and homeward bound.

Roger says he worked as a paper boy in Johnson's and recalls difficulty with the manager who was Mr Johnson's son-in-law. "Doing a paper round from 11 years of age and starting deliveries before 7am, I recall asking for a rise of six pence on top of my eight shillings. After an argument with him, whilst the shop was full of Needle Industry workers, the manager opened the till and threw sixpence at me. It took me five minutes to find it between all those legs in the queue. Valuable experience for later in life I became a trade union negotiator."

For my mum there could not be any shopping if it were wash day and her turn to have the shared washhouse. Firstly, a fire underneath the 'copper,' (large metal tub), was ignited by inserting burning paper and sticks and then coal, after which the tub was filled with cold water.  When this was hot, the clothes were rubbed with hard soap, pushed up and down with a dolly stick, rinsed in chilly water in a metal drum and drawn through the mangle before the items were pegged on the washing line. This washhouse was shared with kind Mrs Shelton and when it was her turn, she would always tap on the door and ask, "Dus yer mam want a bucket of suds?" Mother always reciprocated when she washed, with nothing wasted. Mrs Shelton lived in the first cottage, next to the archway, Ernie Lamb next door, then the Pearson family[5] and finally Ann's older brother Jim!

Mrs Shelton (SLHG).

Also, whilst I was living in this road, I was fascinated by the steam roller regularly parked on the grass island at the junction of Toms Town Lane, Littlewood Green and Crooks Lane, being an area, which was later used as a speedway track. It had a trailer, which was a wooden caravan, complete with a coal stove. The entrance was at the rear and there were wooden steps leading up to the driver's home. I was not allowed to go to see the steam roller at night as I was too young but during the day it was magnificent although noisy. Like other young boys, all I wanted to be when I grew older, was a steam roller driver.

---

5   *Studley Historian*, Issue 16, p.9 and *SH* Issue 24, pp.3-6, 'The Wattons of Studley'.

I have vivid memories of my life in 'the Yard' including a gale which caused a chimney pot to crash into the yard as we looked out of the window. Also, of waking up to find a snow drift completely covering the toilet block, necessitating dad digging an access before the door could be opened. That was the winter of 1947 and I also recall that the family walked down Middletown Lane as far as Coughton Woods to see the most wondrous snow formations I have ever seen in the UK.

Coughton Woods in winter by Roger Thomas.

Thankfully, my father returned from the war, just before my fourth birthday. I was on the pavement by the arch when I saw this soldier in full uniform, walking towards me. It was my dad with a full kit bag on his back, when opened it revealed wooden toys which he gave to Peter and me. There was a metal picture of a panda bear, taken off a vehicle of the division of which he was a part, which sadly was lost. There were happy nights when family visitors came to see him but my world had changed!

Although, of course, I did not realise it then, not everyone's dad was conscripted because of their employment in factories producing equipment needed for war, like

Austin Motor Company at Longbridge, the BSA and Royal Enfield at Redditch. Meanwhile in Studley the 'Needles' were manufacturing machine gun belts.

In the introduction of her book, *The Day the War Ended*, Jacky Hyams says:

"He was a stranger. He lived permanently on the mantelpiece. Like millions of other kid's dads, in the summer of 1945 when World War II ended. My father was an absent presence in our home until the day of his return… 'That's your daddy', children all over the country would be told, families pointing to the man in uniform, proudly staring into the camera…".[6]

Yes! Peter and I were just two of those millions. We were too young to know what was happening as parents did not explain these things to children. "Best that they don't know," parents and grandparents thought. Our world had changed forever and even more so when in June 1946 a woman, stepping out of the doorway, said to me. "You have a little brother." The cottage was too small for a family of five, and this was to take us to Foster Avenue, where I was very unhappy! But more on that story later.

I often returned to see Ann and her mother in the most welcoming kitchen and dining room in a building at the rear of the house which has an attic above, accessible by an exterior wooden staircase. But on one of those visits I saw an ambulance in the road and Mrs Shelton told me to go home. I did not know why there was a problem, nor was I told anything. But as Mary Brazil explains, "Arthur mentioned my mother and following her tragic death when Ann was only nine, I was left to run the family. Demanding times had returned and I cared for my dad until he died"![7]

Mrs Cook At The New Jubilee

Roger says that he remembers the New Jubilee and its proprietor, Mrs Cook, very well and some Saturday lunchtimes.

"I used to take the empty bottles back for a refund to the outdoor (lid hole). Most of the time she would say while giving me a wink 'your dad's over there', pointing to the bar, which he was propping up. I thought she was a lovely person as sometimes I got a bottle of pop and crisps from my dad. One day, me and my two brothers, Gordon, and Dave, got the job of digging and weeding the shrub and flower beds at the Jubilee. I was the only one who enjoyed gardening, so they

---

6   Hyams, Jacky, *The Day the War Ended*, (2020), p.1.
7   *Studley Historian*, Issue 16, p.9 and *SH* Issue 24, pp.3-6, 'The Wattons of Studley'.

left me to it when Mrs Cook's back was turned. Mid-morning while still digging and weeding on my own, Mrs Cook brought out, on a tray, three pints of ice-cold lemonade and lime; sheer luxury in those days. I drank all three pints over the period of the morning as my brothers had not returned. When they did return, they were not happy seeing three empty pint glasses. I remember Mrs Cook paying me extra money, she didn't miss much! One Sunday winter's night my father Maurice was having a drink at the Jubilee and just after closing time Mrs Cook asked someone to go out to the car park to put up the chains which were attached to concrete posts. This was to stop Gerald Golbourne's cows coming across and messing up the car park when he brought them up Middletown Lane for morning milking. Forgetting my father was on his bike and being one of the last to drink up; he rode straight into the chains, over the handlebars and knocked himself out. Recovering sometime later and arriving home covered in blood, my mother who told him off, thought he had been involved in a fight. It did not change my opinion of Mrs Cook; I still thought she was a lovely lady."

The New Jubilee by Roger Thomas.

Hills And Hollows

My story continues by sharing with you the memories of Roger, myself and other Studley residents:

Across the fields of yesterday.
He sometimes comes to me.
A little lad just back from play.
The lad I used to be….
       Thomas Jones Jnr., 1882-1932.[8]

Walking from our cottage was easy and safe, even for small children. Having to cross Node Hill (Bromsgrove Road) was quite easy, as I could sit near Feasey's shop and not see a vehicle for hours! The one exception was in June 1944 when, as far as the eye could see, there were USA military vehicles heading south. Barry Cooper also witnessed this, "I remember convoys of probably new army vehicles, troop carriers I think".[9]

What none of us knew as children when we shouted, "Got any gum chum?" was that this was a movement of USA military equipment from Liverpool to the south coast in readiness for D-Day! For Peter and me, better that we didn't know that our father and thousands of others were assembling there. Mercifully, for us, dad would be in a later wave of troops crossing the channel!

Walking down the lane, the first building on the left was Wilson's dairy, near Roger's home, and he writes, "Frank Wilson, his wife with Ann and Diane, ran a dairy from here, where they kept a lot of pigs which I used to help him with on a Saturday."

As I continued past the houses with unusual façades which we called, "the agricultural houses" we then passed Middletown and along by the front of another of the Peart's farms on the left. It was then I looked for an opening leading to a five-bar gate. This was the entrance to, what we kids, who could not pronounce our 'h's, called the 'ills and 'ollows, and I was just one of many who were inspired by them, including Clive Hill, who says, "I have fond memories of family days out over the Hills and Hollows. We often whiled away our school holidays by

8   Jones, Thomas Jnr., *Sometimes.*
9   *Studley Historian*, Issue 28, pp.16-19, 'Node Hill – On the Edge'.

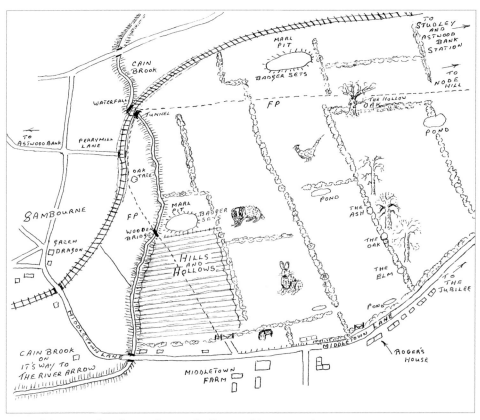

Map of the area referred to in this article illustrated by Roger Thomas.

The Hollow Oak by Roger Thomas.

packing our fish nets, jam sandwiches and homemade ginger beer and going to the Hills and Hollows… In later years I looked down the hills to the stream, not so big now, or is it that I'm not so small?"[10]

I was never alone on my walks, knowing most of the people who lived in the lane, like the Thomases, where I often called to see Roger's brother, David. I am now pleased that Roger is adding beautiful paintings to illustrate this book. Roger says, "Middletown was a different world, over the fields we climbed every tree and could name them all, e.g. 'The Hollow Oak'. Can anyone remember the fields called the Hills and Hollows?"

After our move to Foster Avenue, I sometimes saw the same girls who sang whilst they skipped in the avenue, Barbara, Joyce, Olga, and others, sitting on the gentle grassy mounds, making daisy chains etc. Later in September we might be filling jars with blackberries to be taken to Dyson's shop in the High Street, in return for a few pence!

The small wooden footbridge that crossed the stream, which we called, 'Middletown Brook', took us to this 'different world!' illustrated in the map opposite. The field beyond was quite different to the sloping path to the bridge, as the meadow, except for mole hills, was flat, and appeared to have remained fallow for many years. It was irregularly shaped, with a low hedge and fence on the left separating it from an unmetalled road which continued underneath the bridge and is captured in one of Roger's painting. The road led to Sambourne Green and beyond or, in the other direction towards Quinney's farm and Astwood Bank or the railway station.

Another side of this field was the railway embankment with a low hedge at the bottom and on the third 'side' were the bushes alongside the stream, emerging from the tunnel, gently meandering towards the wooden bridge. To the east of the stream was a large pond at one end of the Hills and Hollows where we might see a moorhen nesting in the centre, safely out of reach from egg collecting boys!

The grass of the meadow was tufted but there were areas where families could picnic quite near to the stream although they would have to watch out for 'cow pats,' as sometimes cows grazed there. These were kept securely within by metal gates, one by the bridge and another attached to a strongly reinforced flat bridge with a low brick wall. This was above the stream, fed through a surface water pipe and laid by railway engineers when building the embankment. On the top was the single railway track between Barnt Green and Alcester and beyond! This

10 *Studley Historian*, Issue 27, pp.14-15, 'Hills and Hollows'.

pipe was a challenge to boys like Roger and me as we both had tried to clamber to the other side of the embankment through the pipe but were prevented from emerging the other side by a small waterfall and brambles, rendering it impossible. It was scary, because at first it was dark and the light at the other end seemed a long way off!

At this point it needs to be explained that my memories span many stages of my life, from early childhood in Littlewood Green, into my years in Foster Avenue then later the High Street. Adventures were shared with many others, including John Shakles; when I was with them, we might dare one another. But, for now, my story concerns when I lived in Littlewood Green!

Wives of service members, having no labour-saving domestic equipment, were quite glad for kids not to be "under their feet." We rarely had a newspaper, did not have a radio and TVs for the likes of us would come much later, so there were none of the 'scare stories' we might expect today. In any event, if there were risks to young children, it would quickly become known to villagers, as mums chatted to one another in shop queues.

So, my wandering off was not a problem if I was not away too long.

Normally I would not have entered the tunnel, not even crossing the bridge. But the bridge was very tempting, as Clive Hill, says:

"We ran down the hill to the stream (but what seemed to be a raging river to us kids) and out came the picnic rug in scenes later reminiscent of the TV versions of Nesbitt's Railway Children". He continues, "When we heard the rumbles coming down the railway track, we scrambled up to wave to the train driver who always blew the whistle to acknowledge us. Dad never seemed to worry we were a few feet away from the train, not so much health and safety in those days."[11]

When I was living in the Avenue and John living in Crooks Lane, we regularly walked there by different routes and sometimes I went alone. On one journey I walked through the field, accessed through a gate at the junction of Node Hill and Middletown Lane where in the far corner was a large pond. The recently harvested corn field meant that I was able to walk diagonally towards the pond and the spinney which surrounded it. But as I approached John Watton, later the husband of Sybil Dyson, jumped out of a tree camp he had built. You might imagine it scared me, but not for long, especially when he taught me how to make an acorn pipe. Taking a fallen acorn, he scooped out the kernel then having

---

11 *Studley Historian*, Issue 27, pp.14-15, 'Hills and Hollows'.

The embankment and train by Roger Thomas.

made a small hole in its base, inserted a stout piece of stubble. I had my first pipe of tobacco which was all part of the growing up process.

When we arrived at the embankment we enjoyed seeing the train and after putting an ear to the track we were able to know if one was approaching. There was the fun of going in and out of the bushes to the stream edge. The stream was shallow but there were deep lagoons where trees had fallen across so kids could safely fish for sticklebacks in separate places and put them in jars of water to bring home.

Roger says of his adventures. "We played on the railway lines, fished in the brook and ponds. Sadly, all the ponds and trees have now gone. Prairie farming! We even made a den down by the brook, known as Spittle Brook. I had a gang which included me, Malcolm Bennett, Chris Gibbs, John Fowler, Ralph Archer and more – all harmless fun."

Many years later with my mum, then living in Lansdowne Crescent, with our children, like the experiences of Clive, we took the path to Node Hill, crossing the road to walk along the edges of fields alongside the 'Hollow Oak Tree', into which we could climb. No trains for them! However, for them there was fun in their wellies, walking and splashing along the stream, where possible, in a situation which seemed unchanged by time.

Doubtless, with me telling stories, about once being able to walk on the left-hand side of the stream to the bridge at the foot of the hill in Middletown Lane and clambering underneath, into the fields on the other side of the road. Also, of our experiences of that part of the stream where, for example at the bottom of a high bank we could get grey clay which, when wet, could be fashioned into small containers and figures etc. If we went a little further downstream by crawling under a barbed wired fence and walking upwards towards Middletown we were in another meadow where Golbourne's dairy cows grazed.

Middletown Brook by Roger Thomas.

Foster Avenue

The arrival of younger brother Dennis in 1946 resulted in the need to move to a much larger house and it wasn't long afterwards that I stood with my mother in the Council Offices at Alcester, (a collection of isolation hospital buildings, in which later I was to begin a career in local government), collecting the keys to No. 4 Foster Avenue. The tenancy agreement prohibited the "keeping of coal and livestock in the bath" and numerous other petty rules. However, No. 4 was a palace. It had 3 bedrooms, fixed bath, toilet upstairs, one outside toilet and our own washhouse, sheds and garden. Rent was collected every week by Mr

Woolnough (later Cliffy Portman), and woe betide anyone who did not pay, with Chief Rating Officer, Eddie Parkes, striding up the front path with leather bound book which was opened for all the neighbours to see.

It is difficult to visualise now how it looked when we arrived but the map below is helpful. Looking at Toms Town Lane, the road just below the Baptist chapel shows the only houses on the Alcester Road end as well as New Road and Watts Road. Then add the 'between the wars' houses from the new Greys Road, around into Toms Town and then continuing the other side of New Road to where Crooks Lane meets Littlewood Green, (not on the map) the addition of agricultural cottages.

The post-war development of Foster Avenue was from those cottages on the same side of Toms Town Lane, just short of Greys Road, then on both sides to the junction with Crooks Lane. Built in phases, the last of which was the centre section. At the time of this development the last few houses to the corner of

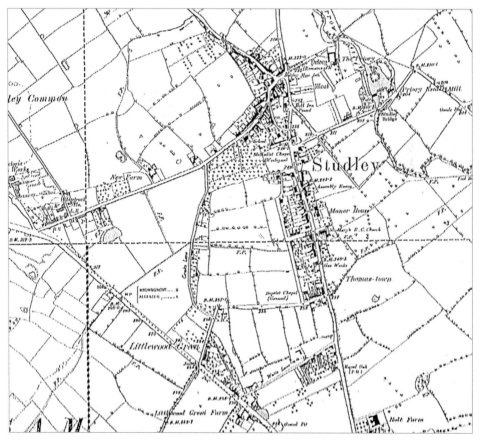

Section from Studley 1901 Ordnance Survey Map (Bill McCarthy archive, SLHG).

Littlewood Green were added. There was a night watchman's hut in this area and we kids were enthralled by the tales told (Uncle Remus like)[12] by old Evan Jones as we sat around the glowing brazier inside this shelter.

Our new home was on the left-hand side of the junction with Toms Town Lane and we were to witness the continuation of the Foster Avenue development, then later the new homes built near Toms Town Lane. Firstly, the building of prefabricated houses between Watts Road and Toms Town Lane, then the building of houses of Allendale and on that side, houses from opposite the junction of Greys Road down to the white cottages and Williams' woodyard at the junction with Littlewood Green.

The "prefabs" were demolished to make way for more permanent dwellings. In this photograph the last "prefab" in Studley is being demolished. The man at the front is Bill Dyson who, when I was a boy, lived in Foster Avenue.

We didn't have much furniture and most of it would have been 'handed down'. In order to move it dad borrowed my uncle Gerald Read's truck, a converted high pram with wooden sides. I helped him move it all, for the 600 yards from one house to the Avenue, taking us along Littlewood Green to Williams' woodyard,

---

12 *Uncle Remus* is the fictional title character and narrator of a collection of African American folktales compiled and adapted by Joel Chandler Harris and published in book form in 1881.

but as we negotiated the bend the double bed almost fell off. Dennis Williams, although laughing, did come to our rescue and stayed with us until we were at our new house. I felt that we had moved onto 'another planet', which I did not like at all, so at every opportunity I returned to my former 'playground' which got me into trouble with my parents many times. One memorable occasion was when instead of going from school to my new house I went to Middletown Brook via the Hills and Hollows. Whilst there I picked some pussy willows, which were growing on the bank, proudly bringing them home to my mum. But dad was not amused, as he had purchased tickets for my brother, Peter and me to go with mum to the Palace Theatre, Redditch. The outcome was the willows were thrown in the garden, me sent to bed with no tea and June Webb from next door taking my theatre ticket!

But after a while I settled in, just got used to it and began to enjoy the things that it offered, most especially the fields that surrounded it, which, before the house building I have described, were our unrestricted playground. The 'Toms Town fields' belonged to Allens, hence the name given to Allendale chosen for the new estate. The field at the top of the Lane did have some barbed wire fencing, but that was to keep in the white shire horse named, 'Captain', not to keep us kids out! Alongside the lane two large trees had been cut down and the stumps were a perfect place for us to feed the horse with dock leaves.

Shire Horses by Roger Thomas.

What are now the school fields of the Studley High School in Crooks Lane and the Roman Catholic infant school in New Road were known as Newlands and in the centre was a public footpath from New Road to Crooks Lane. This was a vast unrestricted playground and when building work began, even better still, we could jump off scaffolding into sand piles and lots of things like that. Gradually I had forgotten Jubilee Yard.

Many of the people who lived in the Avenue worked at the 'Needles', which was the name most Studley people gave to both the Old Factory (Central Works) and the New Factory (Arrow Works) to which they could easily walk or cycle. In addition, there was a huge air raid shelter opposite the Barley Mow which was used for leaving their bikes. It seemed that every adult had a bike and most had been made at factories, like Royal Enfield and BSA in neighbouring Redditch and where many Studley residents worked. Neighbours Mr Bennet and Mr Hale travelled to work on little green motor bikes but there were some who didn't work in any of the factories, like Mr Lichfield, a telephone engineer, Mr Howell, a small farmer at Spernal Ash, Mr Twigg was a lorry driver and Mr Clarke, Mr Preston and others were in the building trade. Terry Shakles mended bikes at his home and his neighbour, Mr Rogers was a welder with a workshop next to the Duke of Marlborough. Barry McTigh, always cheerful, although badly disabled, went to work in a hand-made wheelchair (an upturned bike with large seat and he pushed the pedals with his strong hands).

I only remember one car belonging to Mr Russell while both 'Bocky' Warner and Mr Lichfield drove vans. Weekly, Crow's hardware in small vans, displaying assorted items of hardware on exterior shelves, with a tank of paraffin which many used for heating, visited the road. But, there were coal fires in these new houses, albeit only in the lounge, so the need for coal attracted several different merchants. Also weekly was Dicky Dyson's van, a converted charabanc with shelves loaded with vegetables. It gave rise to a song the girls would sing as they skipped. "Dicky Dyson sells fish three ha'pence a dish" which was rapidly followed by "salt, vinegar, mustard, pepper." Every day we saw Foster Avenue resident Harry Davis with his Quinney's milk float, sometimes that of rival dairyman John Yapp and there were numerous baker's vans. An ice cream merchant visited us, also in a converted coach and I remember that some lollies had sticks with a free lolly offer, that is, if you were lucky. There were occasional visits by rag-and-bone men and it was said that a boy from neighbouring Greys Road gave up his jacket for a balloon!

Of course, we had to go to school which is where I first met John Shakles. The headmistress of the Infants School was kindly Miss Griggs but then, at age eight, we moved up to the C. of E. School, known as the 'Big School'. On Sundays we had to go to Sunday school, which I hated, except when Canon and Mrs Kemp or the 'Grey Lady' (a member of a religious order that wore grey) were there. But there were some advantages, like the Sunday school outings when we usually went to Warwick for the day. Dad used the Coach and Horses pub, next to Dysons, and they sometimes organised trips to Weston-Super-Mare. On those special days we travelled in a charabanc, (another name for coach), filled with adults, kids, beer crates and crisp tins plus, if we were lucky, plenty of a popular bottled drink, Vimto and straws.

We also loved to go to the track-cycle racing event held on the Green, on the corner where Crooks Lane meets Littlewood Green, to cheer our team, Studley Tigers, which included our heroes, several of whom came from our estate, the Kessey twins, 'Kidney' Watton and 'Turk' Wilkes; there was also 'Toshy' (John) Watton from Littlewood Green and 'Poey' Lowe from Toms Town Lane. Every boy in the village had a nickname, not all of which were flattering!

In the summer months, we went swimming down the Park, having our lorry wheel inner tubes inflated at Park Garage en-route and using our favourite swimming holes. Towards the end of summer, it was pea-picking time as we visited various farms earning a few pence per net while in the autumn, it was 'spud-bashing', a back-breaking exercise, which involved chasing the farm tractor and filling sacks with potatoes for extra pocket money. If we were lucky a farm labourer would bring us a bucket of hot chocolate into which we dipped our mugs. Hot chocolate never tasted better.

From the age of nine I went to the Co-op grocers every Saturday morning, to fetch our weekly provisions, all hand served by Silv Canning or Mr Barker. On my return, it was off to my gran's in Castle Road with grandad bringing me back at night. I hated doing that shopping because kids from the 'Toms Town gang' would come out of the trees and tease me, threatening to take the groceries, but then I learnt how to fight so it was OK after that.

We had one shilling (12 old pennies) (5p) per week pocket money and sometimes we would go to the Cosy, then owned by Jack Leuty, for the Saturday matinee priced at 6d, an ice cream at 3d and a bag of chips with scratchings, (small pieces of fried batter), for 3d from the Cosy Corner fish and chip shop. They regularly showed Tarzan and Roy Rogers black and white films. Alec Dyer worked the projector, which was always breaking down, adding to our enjoyment and ushers Mrs Tilsley or Mr Waring had problems controlling us!

Youngsters did part-time work, so from the age of 12, on Saturday mornings, I worked at Dicky Dyson's fish and chip shop in the High Street on the corner of

Marble Alley. When I first arrived at 8am, my job was working with Dicky Dyson's wife, Eileen, putting 'spuds' (potatoes) into a sort of grinding machine, then when finished they were emptied into a large tin bath of freezing icy water. We had to 'eye' them (remove any shoots growing in them), scrape off any remaining skin and put them into another bath of chilly water. We did this until all the sacks of potatoes, which we had to move from the garage on the left-hand side into the work room at the rear of the shop, had gone. Then we both went into the cottage to the right-hand side of the shop where she did cheese on toast for us. Then I took her list of grocery needs and went down to Mason's Grocers, on the left-hand side of Fleece Hill (lower High Street), then across the road to Hunt's bakery (opposite junction of Redditch Road), next back to the cottage and then either home or down to my gran's in Castle Road. My Saturday morning wage was 2/6d (12½p).

I was fascinated by this building and when time permitted would wander down the back to investigate its former stables, whose entrances were in Marble Alley, one of them housed Dicky Dyson's black Austin 14 car. The other was filled with junk, or was it? Just before November 5th, Eileen asked would I like it for our bonfire. You might imagine that, together with Robbie Webb from next door in Foster Avenue and others, we were soon there with borrowed prams etc. Being a corner position, as with next door which was in Toms Town Lane, No. 2 had a large front garden but having a very small rear one. The front garden was perfect for our bonfire which we built away from the house and outhouses. But when 'Webber', as my dad always addressed him, came home, he did not want to damage his prized brassicas, so it was moved nearer the house, which had recently been painted. It was some fire but caused the paintwork on the outhouse gutters and entry door to bubble. However, it was dark and no-one seemed to mind.

The next day as we sifted through the ashes we found useable coins, but what valuable antiques were lost that night we will never know? But Eileen Dyson was pleased to see the back of it. My naughtiness

Dyson's Fish and Chip Shop, which occupied a part of what was Franklin's Bakery, on the corner of the Marble Alley and High Street junction (SLHG).

was well known in the Avenue and I remember screams from the Cowells' and Webbs' girls when I threw water over a wall as they were dressing up for a concert they had organised. I was particularly good at throwing which came in useful at Studley Mop, as I could be relied upon to knock down coconuts. Also, I held the record for the cricket ball throw at Studley C. of E. School in 1953.

Sometime later I gave up the work at the fish and chip shop and on Saturdays worked for my dad as an errand boy but my 10/- (50p) wage paid for my clothes so I had to rely on the generous tips given by some customers for my pocket money.

I began to write this book in 2022 when preparations for the Platinum Jubilee of Queen Elizabeth II had already begun and remembered that 70 years before Studley was celebrating that coronation. I was aged 10 when, at the top of the Avenue, l heard people saying out loud, "The King is dead". That event ushered in preparations for the Foster Avenue coronation street party.

The Foster Avenue Coronation Party, Foster Avenue, Ivy Cooke (SLHG).

In the photograph above you see the Avenue celebration table laid out for us kids. Mrs Foster, of Redditch Road, was in attendance, as the Avenue was named after her husband who was a hardware merchant in Redditch Road. In the photograph you see Sarge Brooks with his megaphone, standing next to Mrs Foster and a side-way view of my dad. Facing us towards the front is Olive Cowell, one of our next-door neighbours and on the extreme right, 'Bocky' Warner.

As most people could not afford a seaside holiday in England and continental ones were unheard of, there was a saying, whenever someone asked "Are you going on holiday this year?" The response was "Yes, to Spernall Duck Races." Or in other words "No." Long after I left the village, I heard that villagers had organised such an event, upstream of the bridge at Spernall and used plastic ducks!

Very few people had television and we were amongst the first in the Avenue. I remember the first thing we watched, on our 12-inch screen Sobell, was Blackpool winning the cup final and seeing their star player, Stanley Matthews. In those days, it was all in black and white and programmes punctuated with interludes, like a bonfire burning or a potter's wheel turned to fashion a pot of some description. The TV needed a huge H shaped aerial attached to our chimney. I remember watching, what for me was the first time, a serialised Nesbitt's Railway Children and this probably explains why I have watched and enjoyed the two different TV versions, in colour, every time they appear!

But in the main we made our own entertainment. We played different games with marbles, one which required a small hole in the turf of the verge then we pitched in the brightly coloured glass balls to see whose would stay. Another involved lining up these marbles against the garden brick walls and trying to hit them with a 'doler', which was a much bigger marble. I have known boys rolling down steel 'ball bearings', which their dads had brought back from the Maudslay factory in Great Alne, where some of them worked.

Also, for indoors we found our own entertainment, although we had begun to receive toys at Christmas, like Dinky cars and painting sets. My brother Peter and I had invented a 'pretending game', which we called 'fort and toolset'. We pretended that we had the sorts of toys our parents could not afford and we slept together in our house in Jubilee Yard. Although in Foster Avenue Peter had his own bedroom, we might still ask of one another, "shall we play fort and toolset?"

I loved using pens and pencils and often got into trouble for using Alcester Co-op billheads for writing paper then, when I could, I bought small exercise books. I invented a farm by using magazines given to the butcher's shop where dad worked. I will explain. Old newspapers were eagerly wanted by shopkeepers so they could wrap up meat etc. From Cleeton's farm, which was one of the clients, we had 'Farmers Weekly' and similar publications. These were no good for the purposes of wrapping food and so I brought them home. With the information inside I was able to 'buy and sell' farm equipment and I kept records of these 'transactions'. All of it whilst I was pretending of course!

As I reflect upon these memories, I realise that this 'game' was to influence the answers I gave during an interview for a place at Alcester Grammar School (AGS). Unlike others I did not pass, which was very disappointing, but the greatest upset for me was that I would not be getting a 'Bayko' building set my dad had promised me if I had passed. But the disappointment did not last too long as I would be invited to attend for an interview. Dad came but, alone I appeared before a panel of school governors and teachers.

I was required to tell them the names and authors of two books I had read, to summarise them and recite some poetry. I could have recited much of 'The Lady of Shallot' but opted for the 'The Village Blacksmith', which a panellist commented upon, because I had told them "What I wanted to be when I grew up", which was a farmer. There was probably at least one farmer on the panel; they were obviously doubtful that I could become a farmer so one suggested that I could be a farm manager. I passed and in September 1953 I started as a new boy at the AGS. I now wonder what they might have said, or done, if I had told them that I wanted to be a steamroller driver.

Studley Tigers

We all looked forward to seeing our team competing with others, like 'The Alcester Lions' and 'Ipsley Imps', on the Green, near to where we lived. These youths took their inspiration from motorbike speedway riding, where teams raced around a track to determine the winner. But this was pedal power, as roadster

Studley Tigers. Of the team, 'Toshy' (John) Watton on the left and 'Poey' Lowe sitting on his bike; the men on the right being 'Bocky' Warner, Jim Watton, an older brother of John and Mr Russell from the Avenue (SLHG).

bikes were stripped of their gears and brakes, converted to 'fix-wheel' with straight handlebars fitted. Later, I think because of road safety fears, the circuit was moved to the recreation ground in Crooks Lane, with its entrance next to Frost's shop.

Studley Mop

In our family, birthdays, other than special ones like age 21, went unnoticed and I do not recall being invited to one. It might have had something to do with what we could afford, but Christmas was quite different when every effort was made for Father Christmas to bring the toy I requested. There were parties laid on by the church and as I mentioned some pub coach trips to various places. Some people attended events at the Canteen or Vicarage Hall. All of this might explain the excitement associated with Studley Mop which was held in the recreation ground whose entrance was alongside Frost's shop in Crooks Lane. It took place in the autumn and by the time we arrived it was usually dark but this added to the excitement.

Over the years it changed in its format many times but my earliest memory is that on the left as you entered the grounds, there were swings on the left-hand side, and these were like little boats where two people sat either end and pulled the swing upwards with ropes, rather like they were bell-ringing. Opposite was a candy store where you could buy homemade sugar fish etc. As you went further into the fair there were hooplas where you threw rings to land completely around the toy you wanted but never could; another where you needed to hook a plastic duck from the water and, if it had the right number on the bottom, you might have won a goldfish in a transparent bag with which to carry it home. Then there were marquees of slot machines, halls of distorting mirrors and lots of trivial things like that, whilst in the centre were the dodgems, which were electrically driven two-seater cars, fitted with bumpers so that you could bump into each other. There was a carousel with music similar to that of an organ, but later this was replaced by the latest pop songs, like Frankie Vaughan's 'Green Door'.

But one year there was something quite different, a cylindrical tank about six foot deep and a ladder leading up a diving platform. Above the tank were the names, CURLY AND MADGE. Also not far away were tents in which it was possible to see some freaks of nature, or were they? I will let Colin, a brother of John Shakles, describe what happened next:

"Once inside a large crowd was gathering beneath a scaffold that was sixty feet high and had a small platform at the top. On the ground beneath was a large circular tank with water to a level of around five feet. A woman with a collection tray for contributions was shouting 'See Curly, the diver, defy the flames.' Curly is not insured someone muttered. Curly strutted around the crowd; a man of medium height in his forties wearing blue tights and a filthy yellow cape. Slowly he began to climb the ladder and reached the platform; the woman assistant threw a full bucket of paraffin onto the water followed by a lighted match! The flames roared, Curly bellowed, did a handstand and launched himself into the air. He landed in the tank, disappeared from sight and then surfaced beating out the flames with his hands.

"We moved on and spotted three tents joined to one another; the first said, 'See the fifty stone woman' so we paid our sixpence and went in. 'Hello lads' said the largest woman I had ever seen; she was sitting on a reinforced soapbox. I don't remember what was on the second tent but nevertheless we paid our sixpence, went in and were shocked to see a tiny woman stretched out; she had no arms just tiny hands protruding from each shoulder. She was knitting a scarf with her feet, the needles firmly clenched between her toes. The third tent was 'See the four-horned ram'. In we went, sixpence duly paid and sure enough, the ram had four horns. Finally, it was time to go although we would have loved some fish and chips; sadly, we had spent all of our money."[13]

Swimming Holes In The 1950s

Whilst living both at Foster Avenue and later in the High Street I swam regularly in the river Arrow. We were forbidden to swim off Castle Road bridge, as two men, Joseph Vale and Caleb Hemming were both drowned there on 5th May 1876, an event never forgotten by older generations who handed down this account. Also, it being near the scouring works of the factory, we often saw oil slicks in the water.

We all knew these pools by name:

No. 1 Seven Steps, popular with young mums and children, being to the rear of Studley Cricket Ground (shaded area), accessible from Manor Road and the unmade Gunners Lane. Perhaps the children might have some crisps or Vimto from the cricket pavilion!

No. 2 Sandy Bend more suitable for older children and those who could swim. It is here that I learnt to swim with the aid of a lorry tyre inner tube, which

---

13 *Studley Historian*, Issue 34, pp.11-12, 'Studley Mop in the 1950s'.

The Waterfall, Castle Road, viewed from the bridge (SLHG).

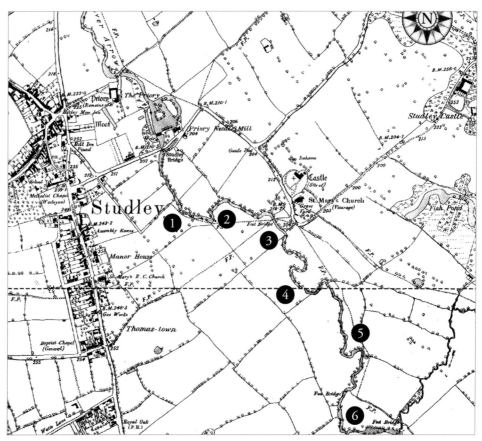

Ordnance Survey, 1901 (Bill McCarthy archive, SLHG).

could be begged from Park Garage and for a few pence vulcanised (puncture repaired) by them! These could be inflated at no cost en-route to the Park.

No. 3 Iron Bridge below the church. The river was deep just before the bridge but then flowed in shallow rapids which were popular for small children.

No. 4 The Blue Lagoon, a straight section of the river and only waist deep but you could float from one end to the other in its fast current. This was pleasant as there were small willow trees planted on either side.

No. 5 The Basin, which was very deep with a steep bank, perfect for acrobatic dives. This is where most of us older lads (10-13) headed, as it was a bit more private and we would light a small fire of driftwood. This was useful for drying off if we only had small towels (or none at all)!

No. 6 The Waterfall was very deep and there was an eel trap there! I remember going there on my own during the period of my GCE exams, but with my dog, Tiny and we used to swim together!

When I think back on some of the things we did I become quite nervous. For example, sometimes when the river was in flood in the early winter, we made 'reed rafts' at Seven Steps and floated down to the Iron Bridge; once all of the way to the Basin, a distance of about one mile.

The River Arrow in flood, at Castle Road weir (SLHG).

In 1958 there were reports that river pollution was the cause of polio which had been suffered by a youth in Redditch. We were banned from river swimming and our fun had come to its end! At this time there was no purpose-built swimming pool in the village, the nearest being on the Batchley Estate, Redditch to which we could cycle. It was primitively covered, but heated, and bathers had their own cubicle at either side. Then a group of volunteers, led by Doug Hill of Foster Avenue, worked tirelessly to raise the funds necessary so that Alcester Rural District Council could build the pool, which is there today.

Our Schooldays

Shortly before John Shakles' illness of dementia became worse and he was unable to continue as editor of SH, we agreed to write an article about our schooldays. Without it this book would be incomplete.

It was at school where our life-long friendship began, two 4-year-olds drawn together by the compulsion of school and mischief! Our mothers may have accompanied us on our first day walking the length of Crooks Lane and then down High Street to the entrance of the Studley Infants School, but from then on, we were on our own. Our older siblings may have been told to keep an eye on us, but we didn't see them. Miss Griggs was the headmistress and the only other teacher's name we remembered was Miss Humphreys whose parents kept a ladies' clothes shop in Marble Alley. The school is little changed except that our toilets were in a separate brick-built structure with a roofless urinal.

As we were so young, a compulsory sleep on camp beds took place in the afternoon, except that we did not sleep but made gestures to one another and giggled. If the weather was good the beds were placed in the playground. If this was all there was to school, we liked it a lot! Each morning (it seemed) we had a tablespoon of malt, sometimes a spoon of cod liver oil and occasionally some cocoa powder, then the nurse would come around to look at our teeth and comb our hair with a nit comb! Sometimes we lined up in the playground for an injection, the doctor using the same needle for us all until it became too blunt and sometimes the mobile dental unit came.

We remember using slate and chalk in our first year in the room next to the assembly hall but by the time we were in Miss Griggs' classroom we had paper, pencils and crayons. We used a shiny toilet paper for tracing pictures and also wrapped it around combs to make a musical instrument. Two pieces of this paper were given to us if we asked "can we go to the toilet with paper?" Sometimes there were games and activities in the assembly hall, and we remember dancing around the maypole! School dinners, for us, were compulsory and the dinner ladies stood over us to ensure we ate them. We remember squirting mashed potato from our mouths at Eddie Sutor whose mother worked there. The food came in huge drums and trays and was horrible as the vegetables were mashed and served with lumpy gravy, while puddings came with lumpy custard. But in the summer, we had the option of sandwiches.

Studley C. of E. School, High Street by Roger Thomas. In the foreground is the headmaster's house before the school with its brick wall enclosed playground.

At the age of 8 we moved to the 'Big School' (Studley C. of E.) next door in the classes, firstly Miss Spillman, then into Miss McCoy, then Mr Montgomery and finally into 'Bully' Evans. Classrooms 1, 2 and 3 were at the school and 4 was in half of the vicarage hall, where a screen separated us from the other class. The headmaster was 'Spud' Taylor and, compared with what is acceptable now, he could be brutally strict with the occasional public caning of boys. We had gardening lessons with Jack Chambers whose liberal use of the measuring rod are remembered. Perhaps some boys did not like him, but he was the teacher who also taught them essential gardening skills.

Two examples of the corporal punishment, I personally witnessed, were given to boys in Mr Montgomery's class, who as a dare, walked through the girls' playground. As well as a boy being publicly caned on the backside before the whole school, as he had thrown a firework in the road outside. In our case it was across the hand and it hurt for days, but one boy, Nicky Ross, immediately went home! However, the following day he was caned, this time on his backside, in front of the class.

Jack Chambers was also a local councillor and very well known to villagers. He often used his teaching position to influence pupils even whilst not at school and perhaps after they had left school. One story, related

The staff of the C. of E. School with headmaster Mr Taylor seated in front row and standing from left to right Mr Cullum, Mr Evans and Mr Chambers.

to me by John Shakles, about an ex-pupil who like John, lived in Holt Road, illustrated this control, or an attempt of control. A motor accident occurred near to Jack's Alcester Road home leaving debris, this boy was walking past along the pavement where Jack stood. He called out the boy's name and said "Go and fetch a broom and sweep up this mess". The boy walked to Holt Road and, out of reach, he shouted back "Sweep it up, your b--- self!" The Jack Chambers I knew, would have secretly laughed at this insolence.

But the class we mostly remember was that of 'Bully' Evans, and who wouldn't? His reputation, like his bent board ruler used to spank boys, was legendary. He had a booming Welsh voice and stood no nonsense. He shared a classroom in the Vicarage Hall.

The building was heated by a coke boiler below and if we finished our sums quickly, we could be asked to go down to stoke it up and add more coke. We knew that if we put too much on, it would lead to scolding water pouring out of a pipe near the main doorway and cause the kids in that part to jump out of their seats and scream. 'Bully' would race down the room, pull one of them through the curtain and shout at them. It was all playful fun, but I'm sure not for that pupil.

The Vicarage Hall by Roger Thomas. The cottages in the Foredraught on the right-hand side.

It seemed as if the older children in that year were in 'Bully's' class and the younger ones in with Mr Cullum, a much gentler teacher. Also, kids from the same street were placed together. We remember in our class, this order of seating: Janet Biddle and Josie Ashley, Jill Latham and Jackie Bennet, Nicky Ross, Josephine Salmonds and Ann Perkins, Charlie Tustin and 'Nobby' (Brian) Clarke, Peter Dyer and Brian Jones, Geoff Hill, Michael Horton and Colin Danks, Janet Heighway and Sybil Dyson, 'Ticker' (Robert) Knight and Terry Sanders, Spencer Tracey and Colin Hale. There were others whose names escape us and to whom we apologise.

There was one incident in the classroom I could never forget. In one corner was a stationery cupboard which housed stationery together with toilet rolls of the shiny paper sort, which were rationed when needed. There stood a classmate, with a toilet roll on his head, dancing up and down and making us snigger. 'Bully' could see his feet moving beneath the open door, went over and slammed it shut, and the fun was over!

Our journeys from school were often eventful. When the gooseberries, which we called 'guzzgogs', were ripe we went via the allotments, to take a few on the corner of Crooks Lane and High Street. When the apples were ready we did the same! Sometimes we went to the Recreation Ground in Crooks Lane and then across Newlands. It was during one of those visits when Mr Bowne's greenhouse suffered some breakages and we suffered 'good hidings' (there was nothing good about them!) Our parents had to pay for the damages.

But the standard of the school and that class must have been good, because a record number passed for the Grammar School and in September 1953 a new adventure in Alcester was to begin!

Many years later I received a copy of the school's sports day report and I was still recorded as having the record for the 'cricket ball throw'.

It is also interesting to read Roger's memories of his schooldays:

"Attending the infant school with Miss Bufton and Miss Evans. I recall a pretty girl with long hair who tied my shoelaces for me, her name was Rylma Hopkins. Getting her to tie my laces, I think, was just a way of getting to know her and it worked. We remained good friends throughout our school days despite Rylma making me sit through the film Hansel and Gretel in the Danilo in Redditch. But being invited to her parties more than made up for it.

"At the C. of E. School in the High Street, no longer there, my friend Malcolm Bennett (Ben) and I were milk and ink monitors; we drank surplus milk and one day when we made the ink from powder and water, we put in too much water. We filled the inkwells and when class started the writing turned out light brown and then disappeared. We never got the job again! Our classroom was the old Vicarage Hall where I recall one day Miss Lane, whose parents had a farm at Coughton, had forgotten the key. I was volunteered to go through an open window to unlock the door from the inside. In the process I caught my trousers on the window catch ripping them from top to bottom as I fell through into the hall. 'Spud' Taylor, who was the headmaster, got his wife to sew me up, I think this was my first pair of long trousers. In a school play I had to carry a dog on stage, the dog, supplied by either Doreen Foster or Doreen Sergeant was large and ran off the stage. The audience was in stitches."

The Park

It seems ironic that this 'industrial village' was completely surrounded by open countryside, but in this short book, I cannot do full justice to it. I can offer a summary of what we had as kids and the overriding factor was our freedom to roam everywhere.

I've shared with you my adventures of going to the swimming holes in the Park, but that was only one small part of what was available to us. There are official paths, one from the Alcester Road to the church, and another from that road but then alongside the Roman Catholic cemetery and out towards the cricket field which also could be accessed via Manor Park Road or along the bumpy Gunners Lane. A path led from the cricket field and then downstream to the iron bridge, another from the iron bridge on a more-or-less straight line downstream of the river which took us to Spernall and probably more. But we were able to wander everywhere from the fence in the Alcester Road and across the whole of this area we simply called, 'The Park'.

As well as the features mentioned there were two former marl pits, one of which was behind the Manor, in Alcester Road, which we named, 'The Valley of Death', as at each end there were steep slopes which were perfect for sledging in the winter snow. None of us owned sledges and had to be content with sliding on our feet or our bottoms. But on one visit some boys found a large sheet of corrugated iron which they curled upwards at each end, making a perfect sledge if you ignore the dangers. The other pit further over towards Green's farm (approximately opposite Holt Road) had a large pond at the bottom, and I remember a time when there was thick ice that we could slide down from the top and across the ice. Boys with bikes would race down these pits and see how far

The Park, the river Arrow, its footbridge, and St Mary's parish church by Roger Thomas.

they could climb up the other side of the Valley of Death or to skid just before they reached the pond in the other pit.

As we got older and became interested in girls, the Park was the perfect place for us to walk alongside the river and to lie down on the bank. Also, for family picnics as the previous painting illustrates.

Walking With John

Later, whilst still living in Foster Avenue, the family of John Shakles moved to Holt Road, which resulted in many new adventures for me, which often took John and I out of the village. As a result of this change, I became familiar with other parts of the village, including Spernal Ash. Villagers would tell you that it was exactly one mile from the Needle Industries (N.I.) Central Works main entrance to Spernal Ash where Adkins, Motor Engineers had a garage, on the junction with Bromsgrove Road. Then, petrol needed to be hand pumped by an attendant, but with so few cars on the road it was never as busy as it is today. Also, at this road junction, there was a telephone box belonging, I believe, to the RAC (Royal Automobile Club) and facing Bromsgrove Road. In those days, long before mobile phones, these were essential for medium or longer distance motoring. There were two such organisations, the RAC and the Automobile Association (AA), both having call boxes for their members, who paid an annual fee and had a key which opened them. Both organisations had motorcycle combinations with essential tools in the sidecar and the rider would salute members as he approached them when seeing their badge proudly displayed on the front grill or bumper bar.

Hilda Richardson (Bill McCarthy archive, SLHG).

Further towards Studley, near the Royal Oak public house, Louise Coopey kept a sub-Post Office and Grocery store.

Just before the junction with Watts Road was 'Red Gates', an impressive house, which faced the Park. It was here that Studley personality Hilda Richardson lived. Always heavily made up and dressed in brightly coloured clothes she was an active charity worker especially for the Darby and Joan, she entertained in the ENTACO canteen. In

Coopey's sub-post office, Alcester Road (SLHG).

those days she could park her Austin Cambridge car anywhere to go from shop to shop and she was always laughing and talking to everyone.

During 1960/61 she talked to parents about the need to recreate a Young Conservatives Group in the village and my dad was one of them. Shortly afterwards a number of us met in the Vicarage Hall and the group was formed, with me being appointed the founding chairman. Its members included my brother Peter, Shelia Hall and Patrick Wainwright.

Our meetings took place in an upper floor committee room in the Conservative Club in Alcester Road and all of those years after the photograph overleaf was taken it looked much the same in 1960/61. Sometime after we left the village it was severely damaged due to an explosion.

It was in that room where we hatched up a plan which was to be my last 'bit of mischief', in Studley. I will tell you more when you read about Roger's experiences at the Studley Castle. My involvement in the Young Conservatives was short-lived as not long afterwards I moved to another job in the London area.

I loved going to John's house in Holt Road which had a large orchard and its own turf covered air-raid shelter that fascinated me. There was a wooden garage and alongside was an open steel water tank into which we might put

Studley Conservative Club, Alcester Road. In the far distance you can see St Mary's Roman Catholic Church (SLHG).

great crested newts which we caught whilst visiting one of 'Scrappy' Watton's yards situated between Alcester and Bromsgrove roads. During one of our adult reunions together in our later years John was fascinated by the fact that I could remember the details of his house, including the arrangement of the downstairs rooms where we sometimes saw his eldest brother Colin who was clearly irritated by us inferior kids.

I'm not sure that John's mum was that keen on me but who was the worst influence on the other was debatable. Sometimes when I arrived at the house, John had already left, perhaps with his younger brother Robert, who we all knew as 'Avro'. Understandably I would try to catch them up but invariably failing so then I had to go in search of my own adventure. A favourite start point for John was alongside Yapp's Dairy in Bromsgrove Road quite near to Golbourne's farm. There was an inviting five-bar gate into a small meadow and then via a track which led to a metal barn where Mr Howell of Foster Avenue kept livestock and stored hay. From there we would make our way towards Middletown Brook as it meandered towards Coughton, where a stream, which flowed from what we called 'Broadmarsh', joined the brook. To explain, 'Broadmarsh' was the very wet and soggy area near the bridge at the foot of the hill in Sambourne, which led to Coughton Woods and beyond.

The only arable fields I can recall were on either side of Middletown Lane until it reached the 'Hills and Hollows', the rest of them were pasture to serve the many dairy farmers in the area. Consequently, wherever we walked there were cows and they presented no problems for us, but we did keep a watch for the bulls, and worked out our exit routes should one of them charge us, but none of them did, being far too interested in the cows.

Calves however were another matter indeed as they were both inquisitive and playful and we sometimes had to get out of their way.

At the point where the stream from 'Broadmarsh' joined Middletown Brook as it flowed towards Coughton was a wood we called, 'Sadlers Wood', into which we were afraid to go as we were told there were wild cats which would attack you. Whether there was or not I don't know as we didn't go in there to find out. But of more significance to us was that at the junction of the two streams the one from Sambourne cut deep into the ground and so it had high sides. Some fun we had was by damming the stream with small logs to cause a sort of reservoir, then hurrying further along the stream and building a more substantial one as we watched the earlier dam collapse. Thus, we would go further and further down the stream until we reached the junction and if we were lucky, we might see the

Inquisitive calves by Roger Thomas.

water over the banks and into the grass alongside. Then we would continue our walk towards Coughton.

If all of this activity made us thirsty it did not matter because also at that junction was a spring which flowed into a trough which the farmer had built for their cows. This fresh water we scooped into our hands as it fell towards the trough and we thought this quite safe, but on one occasion we were stopped by a scout leader who had been watching us. Later we saw their camp, but at the time we were unaware of it. His concern was that he didn't want his scouts to see us do this, in case they did the same. He was quite polite but firm and as he spoke with a 'Brummie' accent, (people from Birmingham were known to us as Brummies), we put it down to his lack of knowledge of our country ways, so carried on walking until we came to the next spring, of which there were many en-route to the river Arrow.

I also remember, when trying to catch up with John, thinking they might have taken this route, but they were not there, so I walked in the direction of the source of the spring to a spinney on the opposite side of the railway track to Coughton station, which was between Studley and Astwood Bank station and Alcester. In there was a stream whose banks were filled with primroses but as I picked them a man, who was working on the railway, shouted at me. I dropped the flowers and ran until exhausted in the direction of Howell's barn, so I was not to see John that day. John and I had previously gone to that spinney and walked through the bamboo like grass, which was between the railway line and the spinney, then along the railway line to Sambourne before returning home.

There were plenty of things for us to do without going over Node Hill if on our bikes we might ride around Brickyard Lane and Green Lane but for a short period only during the 1950s we were attracted to the woods we all called "The Sluff", being our pronunciation of Slough. Then there were two entrances, one opposite Hunts Removals, which later became Allelys Heavy Haulage, and the other through a five-bar gate further up near the Redditch border. There were lots of tracks and paths but whether any of them were official paths we never knew; since no-one stopped us, we assumed we could roam around these as we did elsewhere without restriction. I remember a small sand cliff into which we could burrow and other things like that.

The brickyard was something very different as, understandably, when it was in full operation it would have been most dangerous for children to be there and workers would have naturally enforced that rule, by sending us away. But after it closed one of the pits was attractive to youngsters in search of adventure, this

The brick kilns in Studley Brickyard, Brickyard Lane (SLHG).

included sifting through rejected furniture, etc which was dumped there by a man we knew only as Ben, who kept a second-hand furniture store on the corner of Priory Square. I can recall, as if it were yesterday, walking down Node Hill with John carrying a wall plaque which had a stag's antlers and myself carrying a large leather-bound album, filled with postcards of UK holiday centres. The album has long since gone but I still have some of those postcards in one of my many holiday albums. I also recall having a small pink vanity box with a mirror in its lid. It travelled with me to our new home in 1962. As to what happened to those antlers must remain a mystery, as the last I saw of them was on the corner of Littlewood Green as I headed home and John did likewise.

My First Bike

Every boy's and probably every girl's ambition was to have a bike, but they were in short supply, and most families could not afford them, so if we were lucky, we had 'handed-down' ones, as indeed were some of our clothes. My first bike was one such thing and I vividly recall learning to ride it when I was about seven years of age. My mother chose to teach me en-route to my gran's. We went via Manor Park Road, as it was called then, and into the unmade Gunners Lane. To use the word potholed was to understate its condition, for they were more like craters, it was rough but, on this day, it was mercifully dry. My journey began nearest to the cricket field end and with my mum holding the saddle. I lost count as to how often I fell off, or how many bruises I had, and was still struggling when we got to Castle Road, so mum took hold of the saddle again as we continued down the pavement to gran's. On the return we were back in the lane and by the time we were in Manor Park Road I could ride on my own so there was no stopping me, except that is by my mum, and we ultimately got back to the Avenue. I then recall cycling up and down the tarmacked drives and pavements, between the grass verges of Crooks Lane, oblivious to who else was in the lane.

When I was twelve years of age dad asked what we wanted for Christmas. Both Peter and I said "bikes." This led to a bit of head scratching by dad and then us both going with him to the Post Office to sign withdrawal forms from our savings books. On Christmas Day some large cardboard wrapped packages were brought down by Cleeve Crow who lived in Crooks Lane, and not Father Christmas. But as someone who will always believe in Father Christmas, I am in no doubt that he organised it all!

This bike was a blue Raleigh tourer with straight handlebars and a Sturmey Archer gear switch controlling the gears in the hub of the rear wheel. In the hub of the front wheel was a dynamo which would work both the front and rear lights. Did Father Christmas ever give a Christmas present like this one? I doubt it.

Most of the journeys I made were outside of the village and included regular trips to the swimming pool in Redditch. Together with Pat we often cycled to her parents in Birmingham, on main roads and lesser ones which never put us at risk in any way. The longest trip was with John and others when he suggested we would cycle to Cheltenham via the Cotswolds. His father worked as a delivery van driver for Terry's Springs in Redditch and John had accompanied him there so had some idea of the route we would take. When I returned to our Foster Avenue home quite late my mother seemed very bothered and, at first, did not believe that I could cycle that far, but when I explained to my anxious parents the routes we had followed, was told not to do it again.

Walking From Foster Avenue To Castle Road

My route from Foster Avenue would take me over Newlands (now school fields) into Back (New) Road, via Church Road to Alcester Road. I was afraid to continue along Back Road, foolishly believing that the Old Vicarage was haunted and that a ghost appeared in the round window on the top floor.

The Old Vicarage which, in the 50s and 60s, was the home of the Wainwright family. It was at the rear of the Duke of Marlborough Inn (SLHG).

At the junction of Church Street and Alcester Road I remember the fine building of the Manse now replaced by the houses of Manse Gardens. All I ask, is that you try to imagine what I saw as I turned the corner into the main road, and

The Manse and to the right of this photograph are two cottages and then Redfern's shop, another cottage, and then the flank wall of the Co-op opposite the Manor house (SLHG).

now it is gone, like so many of Studley's fine properties. Mercifully the Manor house opposite remains.

Just a few doors along was Redfern's shop, this, like other shops had not changed, nor their procedures, since the journeys I made with my mother from Littlewood Green all of those years before.

This is what the Co-op looked like in earlier days, and judging by their clothing, perhaps it was the Edwardian period? Its position being opposite the Manor and alongside the fine houses of Alcester Road would suggest this. But this was a long time before I was born and I must return to the early 1950s.

Alcester Co-operative Society, Grocery and Drapery Store by Roger Thomas.

Next to the Co-op was Nurse Idle's house. She was also the school nurse, would peer into our mouths, tell us to clean our teeth and then look for head lice. I remember once going to her for her to stitch my leg, cut by barbed wire around a field where I should not have been.

At the bottom of the hill and opposite Manor Road was 'Bulmer's'. This tiny shop, with its little window, was managed by Daisy Bulmer where she sold sweets and small toys. I remember after the war seeing a large queue outside here and the shop next to the Manor Road junction, as sweets were off ration, for just one day, and villagers were taking advantage. I must confess that the Bulmer's suffered from (now I think about it, awful) pranks from young boys, who might say "Can I have some kick me over the counter drops please", which guaranteed them being chased out of the shop! Next and standing back from the road was Williams' Boot Repairs and after a row of cottages was Doctor Fitzmaurice's surgery. Dr Wilfred Joseph Fitzmaurice MB Ch. B. Birm., and Medical Officer of Health, to give him his full title, lived with his family of three daughters, one of whom tragically died as a teenager, in this fine house where he also had his surgery. There was a waiting room to the right-hand side of the house where the system had not changed, patients would move in a 'musical chair' fashion until they were next to his practice door waiting for him to shout, "next please". There was also a door for his assistant Dr Mulvaney, who older residents would avoid as these villagers did not like change! But 'Doctor Fitz' was the old-style family doctor with whom my large family had many contacts. On the day he vaccinated me, he told my mother that he was then off to a house "where 8 children would be sitting round the table". That patient was distant cousin, Janet Sollis (née Blick) from Watts Road. Dr Mulvaney told my father that Dr 'Fitz', as he was known, advised him to be careful of what he said as these villagers, "are all related to one another."

Sometimes I would continue walking to the top of Castle Road but on other days I turned into Manor Park Road and along Gunners Lane, which was then a dirt track, where Stokes had a builders' yard and on the corner was the farmhouse of Miss Richards. As I gained confidence I might instead of walking along Back Road, continue along Toms Town Lane to its junction with Alcester Road and past the Bricklayers Arms, which is now The Lark. In those days you could not buy alcohol in shops and like most pubs it had an 'off-licence', which was a small counter in the passage, where we might buy crisps and a Vimto drink.

A few buildings along was young Tom Allen's butchers' shop and next was his father, Edwin's grocery. He was a councillor, and when I started work at the Alcester Rural District Council, one of my jobs was to deliver Council papers to him. I remember that he would peer over his half-framed glasses and now I think of him as being like, Dicken's 'Mr Pickwick'.

At the bottom of the slope was the Redditch Gas Co. showroom and office. In its yard was a gas holder and it was here that villagers could buy coke for their fires which was a by-product of town gas manufacture. You could buy gas stoves and wealthier customers could pay their bills, although most had pre-payment meters. Further along the road at the back of a house was a workshop owned by Bill Tucker who recharged accumulators. These were glass vessels filled with acid,

Allen's butchery and grocery shops (SLHG).

which provided electrical power for wirelesses in those homes, like my gran's in Castle Road, which were not connected to the electricity supply until years later. Gran trusted us to carry them, but we were warned "don't you dare drop it."

I soon came to the Duke of Marlborough, sadly now lost to the village. It was the positioning of pubs in this road, and then continuing to Gorcott Hill near Mappleborough, which encouraged this little rhyme:

The Duke of Marlborough rang the Bell
At the Barley Mow to tell the Boot
To kick the Dog in the Hollybush.

Another fine building lost to the village was the Vicarage, surrounded on three sides by a spinney but at the back were formal and vegetable gardens which, in Canon Kemp's time as vicar, were tended by a Mr Lee. The war memorial and the Vicarage Hall are all that remain; both have played an important part in the community life of Studley. I will share my memories of the war memorial towards the end of this book.

The Duke of Marlborough, Alcester Road. On the right is the junction to New Road (SLHG).

The Vicarage by Roger Thomas.

32 Castle Road

Another advantage of living in Foster Avenue and now being older, meant that I could walk to my gran's in Castle Road.

No. 32 was the second house up in the terrace you see below. All of these two bedroomed houses in this terrace were the same, each having a small garden and brick laid path at the front with a low brick wall with wooden gate. The front door was rarely used as the 'front room' was kept for best and we children were never allowed in there!

Access to the back door was by means of a passageway between this terrace and the one above. Then the brick path led to all of the rear doors and into the kitchen/living rooms. There was neither bathroom, nor hot and cold water in the houses but there were brick-built washhouses in each backyard, and next to them a lavatory and a coalhouse. There was no piped water to the houses or outhouses but water was drawn from a cast iron water pump which served all six houses.

But this is a description of the house and what made it the family home which we all loved so much was the welcome we received when we walked through that back door! "Duss yere want a cup of tea?" my gran would ask as she turned around slightly in her un-upholstered Windsor chair alongside the fireguard of the black

Castle Road, circa 1930 (SLHG).

leaded grate. In the winter months, when there was a blazing fire, you would hear the whistling of the kettle on the hob as you arrived. When cousins Doreen and Margaret get together, we automatically talk of "our gran". In addition to the many memories we relate to one another, one of us always asks, "Can you remember the way gran drank her tea?" Yes, quite normally she poured the tea from the pot into a strainer perched on the cup, then proceeded to pour it from cup to saucer and blow it before drinking from it. We never asked her, "Why?" and, if she was once short of milk, she would have blown it cooler, but we will never know. Gran was monetarily poor compared with modern standards, but when given money by my grandad she religiously put the rent money and other essentials safely out of sight only using the remainder for other things. There were always some blue bags of sugar and packets of tea in the cupboard.

After we moved to Foster Avenue, I went there every Saturday morning and gran would say, "Ave yer seen our Dos?" referring to my aunty Doris, who had moved to Toms Town Lane shortly after our move to Foster Avenue. She would ask the same question of everyone who came, until my aunt arrived.

The lavatory had a bench with a hole in the centre and below this was a bucket which was collected each week by men who carried it and emptied it into a trough at the rear of a petrol driven tanker parked in the road. The bucket was returned and put back under the bench. Hanging on the wall were torn sheets of newspaper as toilet rolls were not available at prices my grandparents could afford.

At the rear of the house was a long strip garden and on either side of two garden plots were ash paths, from compacted ash taken from fireplaces. Grandad was a good gardener and he had divided his garden into four sections. In one part he dug small pits into which, when necessary, the lavatory bucket was emptied. In the next he had erected a fenced area in which he kept fowl. The other two were used either for root crops or brassicas, and these were alternated, as the others were 'fertilized', over the years. Thus, in this way he could provide all of the eggs and vegetables needed by the family. Also keeping fowl was uncle Gerald, who lived two doors away. These, like grandad's, were bred from day old chickens which could be bought from Johnson's in Alcester Road and were reared in a small run with a paraffin heater in front of the fireplace. Once they had grown into pullets they were placed in the hen run and the small shed grandad had built from wooden boxes. He had also built a much larger shed at the end of the yard in which he kept his garden and other tools.

Sometimes he bought a small piglet from Green's farm at Mappleborough which was kept in a small part brick, part wood, sty and small fenced run. When fully grown the pig was slaughtered, its bristles burnt off on a fire of burning straw, cured and hung in two halves in the living room. Gran would slice parts off it as required and toast it over the fire. This was a special treat for us kids as we watched it toasting and then watched the dripping fat skilfully caught on a slice of bread. The blackened sandwich was then placed into our hands. We would sit at her Formica topped table in the living room and there was never a treat quite like those blackened bacon sandwiches. The only comfortable chair in the room was grandad's armchair which faced the rear and into the yard beyond, but that was reserved for when grandad got home. On the linoleum covered floor there was just one 'peg rug', handmade from an old coat and sacking.

One of the things that we loved the most, that is as well as the toasted bacon, was for gran to tell us stories about the family history. She would tell us of her natural father who ran away rather than marry her mother, and how whilst working on a building site in Birmingham he encountered arsenic and died. Every word of that account I was able to prove when I began family history research years later. I learnt that he died at his father's home in Littlewood Green. When we went to the churchyard with gran, to tend to her youngest son's grave, she would show us the unmarked grave alongside it. Sadly, her son Dennis died before his twelfth birthday and gran mourned him until her own death in 1962, shortly after Pat and I had left the village.

Of special interest was her wine making. Gran did not have sophisticated equipment like demijohns etc. but used a simple enamel bucket with a breadboard on top. The yeast was placed on a piece of toast and floated on top of the mashed-up fruit, or vegetable and water. She made three different wines of carrot, parsnip and elderberry. The first two items dug from their garden and for the third she relied on us kids picking the over-ripened berries, which we got from the adjoining field or, if she did not know, from the back of the scouring works just over the bridge.

The first two were sweet wines which she bottled to be ready for Christmas, although she did not celebrate that event, as two of her sons, Dennis and Charlie were ill and died during winter months. At Christmas there was never any sign of celebration, not even cards on the shelf. Whereas the elderberry wine was unsweetened and had a particular role to play which we grandchildren sometimes had to take a part in.

Grandad was one of the married men, over the age of forty-five, who was conscripted in 1916 due to the dreadful loss of lives, most especially in the Somme. However, he did not go to the 'front', where the majority of the casualties occurred, but joined the Royal Artillery, and his unit joined up with the Indian army in their role of protecting the Red Sea. My gran called the place, 'Aden' and the 'white man's grave'. Understandably she never thought she would see him again when last photographed with him with his family in a Redditch recruiting office. But thankfully he did return in 1918, although granny said, "I thought he had cum 'ome to die", as he was so frail, only half his 1916 weight and suffering from malaria. Sadly, he was unable to work for three years. Of course, all of this happened before the period of this book, but it helps to explain the events in gran's cottage.

Periodically, grandad had attacks of malaria and this is when the elderberry wine came more than useful. Gran would know the early symptoms of shivering and tell one of us, "goo up to Florrie's and get a jug of beer". Off we would go with a china jug to the Shakespeare and in exchange for two or three pence return with the jug filled with draught beer. By this time, the shivering had got worse and grandad was unable to shake the quinine tablets from the jar. Gran, as she had done so many times before, mixed the wine with the beer and brought it slowly to the boil in a saucepan either on the gas ring or over the open fire. Once hot this "Otted", as it was known, was drunk by him and he was off to bed. Unless this was a Saturday, he would be off to work the next day, so if the weather were fine the mattress would be drying in the sun and the bedclothes drying on the line.

Sitting in the lounge of our Essex home I find it difficult to believe that my grandparents could manage to do the everyday things in such a small living room. Since their front room was the "best room" and not normally used, the living room was the only indoor space available for the daily chores. Like the one room we had in Littlewood Green the door opened directly into it and the areas required for the stairs, the fireplace with its protective guard and the gas cooker, left little floor space for the table with stools underneath and grandad's armchair.

But as I explained it was always a very welcoming home and somehow, we all managed. Underneath the staircase in a sort of alcove my gran had her prized piece of furniture, a chaise-lounge which once belonged to her mother, but that usually had things placed upon it. Underneath its head was a large cardboard box containing my matchboxes, cigarette cards and elastic bands which grandad had brought back from the factory. These were, exclusively, my toys and family members would put boxes and cards in there after they used the matches and bought packets of cigarettes. These were my pretending toys and included building bricks, horses and soldiers. From the moment I arrived, until the time

I went home I played with them. Imagine how crowded it became when gran's stepsisters came to do 'spitting'.

Gran had four stepsisters, but no-one would have used that word. They were sisters, aunts, and great-aunts, but unlike my gran, named Annie, they had the names of flowers, which were Daisy, May, Violet and Rose. Daisy did not come to gran's as she was too busy working in the small garden centre in Crooks Lane, which she and husband Harry Westbury owned. Before their arrival brown packages of 'double needles', i.e. pointed at both ends with two connecting eyes in the middle, arrived. Their job was to spit them, by pushing metal spits through the eyes and then repackage them ready for return to the factory, for guillotining into separate needles for the next process. As they did this, they talked between themselves while I lay on or crawled along the floor. I still remember the conversation in what I call "old Studley talk" although my grammar school headmaster called it slang. However, he didn't understand children yet alone old folk.

I will give just one example of part of a conversation generated by my aunty Rose. Referring to her husband, Reginald Pinfield, she said, "Air Reg went to work without his coot and it was rening", to which my aunt May responded "I gut to Anover." To understand this dialect, I need to explain that "gut" was "go to" and "Air" would be emphasised as would "coot" and "rening". Other words for "Anover", being a place, they had heard of but which they could never go, were "bedlam" or "atton", both being asylums. We also must remember that Studleyites did not always pronounce their "h"s. At the rear of this book is a list of words I heard from these and other conversations at No. 32.

As well as my indoor enjoyment I had next door and what we called, "The Plantin". This word is how my grandparents would refer to a plantation and this was within the adjacent field, as illustrated in this map.

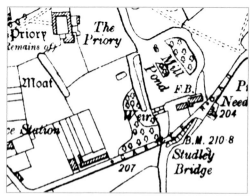

The plantation was the area shown with trees near the Weir, to the north was a long trough, then overgrown and at the top right corner was the remains of a lock, about two metres high. On the left was a large mound and then halfway down the trough was a smaller lock that led into a stream, with another lock before the stream reached the

Extract of the map of 1906 (Bill McCarthy archive, SLHG).

50

river to the east. We understood that these were fishponds belonging, at one time, to the Priory. On the eastern side of the river at the back of the factory, then the Needle Scouring Works, and forbidden to us, (but we still went there!), were similar features but without grazing cattle, it had become extremely overgrown! A piped stream ran from the back of the Works underneath the road, a smaller bridge, under which was constantly running water and returned to the river as shown. Of course, we did not realise that these were 'swan pools', reservoirs which saved water, to provide a constant flow when the working of mill wheels was needed. To us, it was a play area, like those in New Road, Toms Town Lane and the Park.

Afterwards it was back to "me gran's" and after I had my tea of bread with homemade jam gran would say to grandad "You better take that lad home." Off we would go, he pushing his bike, me following behind, but getting close to him as we passed the Old Vicarage! He would knock on our front door at No. 4, my mum would let me in and off he cycled to his local, the Railway pub in Station Road, although gran always called it "The Common".

The Centre Of Studley And Needle Manufacture

The Central Works of the Needle Industries dominated the village centre and unsurprisingly this was Studley's administrative centre for communication and shopping as well as being the cultural and entertainment heart of the village, in its many forms. Both the police and fire stations, the telephone exchange, two banks, the post office, the cinema and the factory canteen were here. As were the major bus stops and main shops.

From the photograph over the page you can see the physical domination of the 'Needles' Central Works. Its head office was opposite the Police Station, Alcester Road, where Sarge Brooks would have been in charge and mercifully those buildings, although no longer part of the police force, have survived the planners' destruction of so much of Studley's heritage.

I remember as a small child going up to the Cosy Corner early in the morning, perhaps on an errand, seeing buses lined up outside Thompson's Brewery waiting to take factory workers to Austin Motors at Longbridge and various Redditch companies. On the other side by the bus stop, buses were waiting to take workers to the Maudslay factory in Great Alne. On this untidy corner, off Bell Lane, stood the green wooden building of Geoff Hill's fish and chip shop. After the Saturday afternoon cinema matinée, we would get a bag of chips and

The Central Works, Alcester Road. On the left-hand side in the foreground is the Bell public house and above the pub you can see the tower, where at the end of the war, a guy was hanged. The road to the right is Birmingham Road (SLHG).

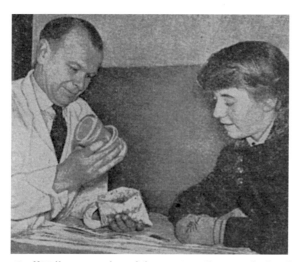

Geoff Hill serving a bag of chips to Ann Skinner who lived in Birmingham Road (SLHG).

'scratchings' for 3d (1p +) and I still remember clawing the last few chips out of the vinegar sodden newspaper; they were delicious!

Because of my passion for chips my cousins referred to me as 'Chippy' and joked that my granny made chips for me and not for them.

The Central Works was commonly known as the Old Factory, or amongst older employees, The Fleece, as it

John Thompson,   BELL BREWERY,   Studley.

An earlier photograph of the brewery (SLHG).

was formerly an inn at the bottom of Fleece Hill, (now lower High Street), which was converted for needle manufacture long before my time. Thompson's brewery was to the left of the Bell public house.

The Central Works together with the canteen and the brewery occupied the whole of the triangle sided by Alcester Road, Fleece Hill and Marble Alley. In the Alley was a green, six-foot-high corrugated fence, with a gate, from the Fleece to the gates of the boiler house and the factory work's canteen.

But firstly how, in the 1950s and beyond, was a needle made? We need reminding that there were numerous types of needles and pins made in Studley. Examples were those for gramophones, knitting, safety pins, darning and embroidery needles. But the ones I know most about are

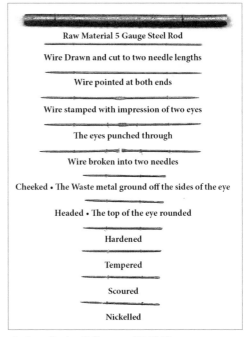

Raw Material 5 Gauge Steel Rod

Wire Drawn and cut to two needle lengths

Wire pointed at both ends

Wire stamped with impression of two eyes

The eyes punched through

Wire broken into two needles

Cheeked • The Waste metal ground off the sides of the eye

Headed • The top of the eye rounded

Hardened

Tempered

Scoured

Nickelled

Arthur Cooke Collection (SLHG).

sewing needles. The diagram on the previous page helps to explain the eleven stages of making a sewing needle from a piece of wire.

A newcomer to Studley would find it difficult to believe that the manufacture of needles in Studley was once comparable to the manufacture of best cutlery in Sheffield. They would also find it difficult to appreciate how the 'Needles', not only dominated the centre of Studley, but the villagers themselves and they might be likened to the folk of coal mining communities. For example, in my gran's house there was never a day when the subject was not mentioned and I consider myself fortunate to have been there to watch her and her half-sisters, sitting around the kitchen table talking as they were 'spitting' needles. Gran was classed as an outworker and the money received was necessary to 'keep the wolf from the door', as she used to explain. But it was not only what they were doing with their nimble fingers, so essential for these later stages of needle production, it was the conversation about what was going on in the factories.

My late wife, Pat, worked in the needle inspection department at the Arrow Works which we all called the New Factory and these were her reminiscences:

"In 1956 I moved, together with my grandparents from a farm in Cubbington, Warwickshire to 36 Birmingham Road to provide a home for my widower uncle 'Son' (Alfred) and my cousin 'Annah' (Anthony) Fitter. The tenanted house belonged to St Vincent's Homes, who owned the Priory and Field Farm where my uncle worked. The teenage orphans lived at the Priory and were taught farming skills, in readiness for emigration to countries like Australia.

"Before this move, I worked in a departmental store in Leamington but there were no such opportunities locally so like most 15-year-old girls, I got a job at 'the factory'. I remember the interview with Miss Ingles and nervously spilling needles all over the floor as I tried to 'head' them. Our equipment consisted of a palette knife and a finger pad of chamois leather. Our 'stage' was the last before the needles were packaged for retail sale and we received them in small brown parcels. We had to roll them, then with the leather, catch the points and turn them (heading) so that they lay in one direction. Then with a needle we checked for those with broken eyes and other imperfections. After this process and using the knife, they were placed back in the parcel, tied, and handed in for reinspection. Despite my initial 'spill' I was offered the job, and although still reluctant, I quickly adapted to the work and made many friends with the inspection girls, those from Studley including 'Tye' (Brenda) Bryson and Janet Blick as well as several from Alcester and Redditch, some of whom I am still in contact with.

"Victorian attitudes towards factory girls remained and supervisor Madge Clark kept us in order. She did not like us talking and if we laughed (which we often did!) she reported us to her boss, Walter Griffin, who worked in an adjoining office. Also, if we needed the toilet, we first reported to Nurse Morris who gave us two sheets of hard shiny lavatory paper! But the real incentives for us was that this was piecework and wages were only paid for those parcels which were accepted after reinspection by Rosie Dyer. If she found rejects the whole parcel had to be re-inspected. Also, we had to work a week-in-hand and there was no holiday pay. So, in the two weeks before the main holiday we worked especially hard to ensure that we had pocket money and these weeks, like those before Christmas, were known as 'pudding weeks'. The lucky few were also able to bring the needles home for inspection and this outwork supplemented our income. The needles in their various stages moved around on large trolleys between the various factory 'shops' and one of the 'trolley-pushers' was Charles Cooke, an extremely popular man who was always cheerful and despite his age (late seventies) never showed any tiredness! On 31st August 1962 I left the factory for the last time. The next day I married his grandson Arthur and we went to our new home in the London area."[14]

Coincidently, Nurse Morris was Roger's aunt May, and the Thomas family visited her every Sunday. He recalls that when ill in bed she asked him. "Are your bowels working?" and he thought she said, "are your bells working?" which he did not understand. He also remembers when she herself needed nursing care, following an accident when the brakes on her bike failed whilst cycling down Fleece Hill and finishing in hospital with a broken collarbone. In better times he often travelled to Evesham by train with her and as they travelled along, she would keep saying, "fish and chips, fish and chips", to the sound of the wheels clicking as they rode over the gaps in the railway lines.

The New Factory in Birmingham Road is still there but used in vastly different ways. Some time after I left the village the whole of the Central Works was devastated by a major fire. This fire, in my mind, symbolised the end of an industry in which countless members of my family worked. It is something I cannot come to terms with. All of this was long after we left the village but I still have those lovely memories. Now it's gone but, in my mind, this was the Studley of my boyhood which was still there when I waited to catch the 148 bus to take me to Alcester Grammar School.

---

14 *Studley Historian*, Issue 20, pp.3-4, 'Needle Inspection'.

Midland Red 148 at Bell Corner (SLHG).

This bus stop was an important 'staging post' for the 148 Midland Red, Birmingham to Evesham service. In the coarse fishing season, anglers who had travelled from Birmingham would leave the bus and join the driver and conductor for a break at Joan's Pantry, owned by Geoff and Lil Biddle but managed by Marion Stock and her attractive daughter Angela. Here people sat at tall stools around the counter and after the break passengers and crew got back on the bus to resume their journey. The bus stop was also a gathering place at night for teenagers and where youths would show off their riding skills (and all too often, the lack of them) on their motorbikes! It was where boy met girl and both were regarded as much as a nuisance as they would be today! Joan's Pantry was the middle of three shops. On one side was Harry Rose's wool shop, where we might go to collect gran's knitting wool. But Mrs Rose was always untrusting of us so watched our every move whilst Mr Rose or their assistant, Mrs Horton from the Wapping, were serving. On the other side was Tommy Davis, hairdresser, who was very professional but this excitable Welshman, who liked his beer, did fall out with some villagers. There were rumours that he had an argument with Dicky Dyson during his very 'short back and sides', shaving him one side and then refusing to do the other!

After these shops were gardens, then Owen's grocers and then the 'new' post office run by Mrs and Mrs Haynes with their daughter and son-in-law. At the back of their confectioners was the PO sorting office where the outgoing post was stamped 'STUDLEY'. I remember my Uncle Charlie Steer being a postal worker there.

Next was a recreation area with two benches facing one another, an ornamental wall and either side entrances to the car park of the NI staff, some with covered spaces. Then came Timothy Whites and Taylors, which was the only place where one could get a prescription in the village and then Huin's Shoes. Following on from there came the 'old' post office, Johnson's ironmongers, to which I have already referred when talking of Roger's employment there. Finally, were two cottages and then Foster's hardware shop, a sort of Aladdin's Cave of crockery and cookware where my aunty Hilda Blick worked.

There were at that time two youth clubs, both on Friday's nights only, one at the Methodist chapel and the other at the Vicarage. The first one was managed by Mrs Murphy of Foster Avenue and Miss Danks from Green Lane. They persuaded me to become a committee member and to go to the chapel on Sunday, but my gran did not approve "you are Church of England" she said. Next to the chapel was a hairdresser, then L.T. Phipps Cycles which later became George's, next was Midland Bank and then cottages, which had long front gardens to the road, which were followed by Bonham's children's clothes later run by teacher Jack Chamber's wife, Hilda. It seems impossible now that just further on was another bank, this one being Lloyds Bank. Next in 'the dip' was Reeve's confectioners which was quite distinctive having a huge ice cream cone outside!

Studley Police Station

The fine building, adjacent to the junction of Bell Lane and opposite the Bell public house remains, but sadly for the village its residents, the two local police officers do not. That situation changed during my twenty years, but certainly when I was a younger child there was both a sergeant and a police constable along with an office, which I once visited when finding a ten-shilling note (10/- now equivalent to 50p). I think the officer may have preferred for me to keep it, as he had to record the details in his register, but that is what my gran had told me I must do. As no-one claimed the note, the officer returned it to 4 Foster Avenue and it was paid into my Post Office Savings account.

This story reflects what the village was like in those days, with most fearful of being the wrong side of the law. This was one of the many advantages of everyone knowing one another so 'naughty' people were quickly identified and quickly dealt with! Most kids, like me, were afraid of being caught doing something wrong because dads would then 'sort us out'. There was little point complaining of a school punishment when we got home, for fear of having more. Incidents in my life illustrate this. Once I was stopped by a police officer in Marble Alley on my late return from Coughton when the dynamo front lamp on my bike failed. The conversation was short. "Who are you?" When I told him, he said "Do you want me to tell your dad?" The other took place in our house whilst listening to Sarge Brooks, who in my early years was stationed at and living at the Police Station. Jokingly although, I think honestly, he told my parents that the way he dealt with these 'young hooligans', was to hit them with his folded cape, as it did not leave a bruise!

Yes, we did hear of lads from the village being sent by the Courts to a borstal prison, which were designed to deal with young offenders. There were also three fifteen-year-old boys, who I personally knew, who had to go to court, having committed a potentially very serious traffic offence. Namely taking one of the Needle Industry's three-ton trucks from its garage and going for a ride towards Stratford-on-Avon. Problems began for them when they ran out of diesel and the garage operator became suspicious as they requested a small quantity of fuel which was rationed because of the Suez crisis of 1956! I was told by one of the offenders that they were fined and their school was informed which resulted in them appearing before the headmaster but not 'swished' (caned on the backside).

A lesser form of mischief I witnessed and laughed about was a group of boys lifting off the police station pedestrian gate and carrying it down to the public conveniences adjacent to the traffic island. The officer, for all his investigatory skills, never found out who the miscreants were!

Studley Fire Brigade

Sadly, in this case, the fire brigade as well as its station in Bell Lane, has gone. My first memory of these brave men, who performed this vital service to the village and beyond, was seeing them on top of the fire engine and dressing ready to go to a fire. This was outside the station on one side of the Swan Inn, High Street, which later became a bowling alley and there was another engine garaged in another building, on the other side of the pub, later demolished to make way for a car park. In those days they were alerted by the siren on top of the tower at the Needle Central Works, in addition to telephone calls to their place of work.

Studley Fire Brigade outside the new station in Bell Lane (SLHG). Howard Vale MBE is third from left side.

The fire station was known as a retained fire station as its crew were all volunteers with their primary aim to extinguish local fires but often called out to assist other brigades. In addition, they did a lot of community work, such as the annual flower show, raising money for the fire officer's benevolent fund which was very popular with villagers, whether as contributors, like Mr Crump of the High Street, whose garden produce often won certificates, or those wanting to watch or take part in the auction which followed.

Howard Vale MBE[15] who I have highlighted in the photograph above, married my wife's sister, consequently I got to know the crew and their valuable work for the village.

Studley Telephone Exchange

On the corner of Marble Alley was the Telephone Exchange, which was staffed by Mrs Ross, who was probably the most informed person in the village! The telephone number of Dad's Co-op butchers' shop was STU 10 so when I rang

---

15   *Studley Historian*, Issue 32, pp.11-12, 'Studley Fire Brigade'.

Hardwick House, which I think was STU 8, I nervously turned the winder on the wall mounted phone and a voice asked me "who do you want?" When I told her she replied, "Mrs Whitehouse is at the hairdressers and won't be back until 12". That was the voice of Mrs Ross!

Formerly an extension of the Alcester Grammar School and later housing the telephone exchange as well as the residence of the Ross family (SLHG).

The daughter of Mrs Ross, Juliet Ives, explained, "The exchange was situated unobtrusively in a quite imposing house called 'Rosedene' (formerly the site of Studley Grammar School), which stood back from the road, on land between the Foredraught and the bottom end of Marble Alley. (We were told that the reason for this unobtrusiveness was to lessen the risk of sabotage by terrorists. Some things don't change.) The telephone switchboard was in the front part of the house, with living accommodation at the back and upstairs. My mother was one of a band of unsung heroes known as Caretaker Operators, usually found in small village exchanges. She was required to be in charge of the switchboard between the hours of 8pm–8am every night and all day on Sunday, an astonishing 96-hour week. She and my father had to undergo a period of GPO (Post Office) training. In May 1956 we moved into Rosedene and prepared to assume the burden of Studley's nocturnal telecommunications. In order to be able to give my mother a break, I soon learned how to operate the 'board', and did a regular shift two evenings a week and Sunday afternoon. My father, too, did a regular stint, and one evening when things were rather quiet, he sneaked into the living room to check on the progress of West Bromwich Albion in a highly important match. Unfortunately, the Albion must have been very boring that evening, for my father fell asleep, to be awoken an hour later by a GPO engineer banging on the door, having been alerted by the Police, who feared that the Studley operator had collapsed and died at the board. 'Listening in' was, of course, most strictly forbidden. My mother, having been born, raised, and educated in Studley, worked there until her marriage and knew practically everyone on the Studley Subscriber List. Not only knew them, but knew most of their family histories, too. It was not for nothing, therefore, that we were all required to sign the Official Secrets Act, forbidding us, on pain of imprisonment, from revealing anything we might just happen to overhear, accidentally, of course…".[16]

In my introduction to this item, I referred to Mrs Whitehouse, who lived in the fine countryside home, Hardwick House, just further along Castle Road and past the Castle gates, near Outhill. Mrs Whitehouse was very involved with the Studley branch of the Royal British Legion and, as Dad was its secretary, they were often in contact with each other, as well as the Co-op supplying her meat requirements.

I went there with my dad at times and was fascinated by what I saw including a cage in which she kept a monkey. Villagers often saw Mrs Whitehouse in the village with the monkey on its lead but sitting on her shoulder. I learnt that she often went into the Bell PH and its patrons watched as she fed the monkey with peanuts. Yes Mrs Whitehouse, like Mrs Richardson, of whom I have earlier referred, was one of Studley's leading personalities.

The Cosy Cinema

There were three places of entertainment within the centre of the village, the Cosy Cinema in Bell Lane, the Vicarage Hall, off the Foredraught and the Canteen.

It is difficult to imagine as you look at the houses in Bell Lane and in Vale Close, that this was once a centre of entertainment. Every town had at least one cinema (or picture house as they were known). Redditch had three and most of

---

16 *Studley Historian*, Issue 19, pp.5-7, 'Studley Telephone Exchange.'

The Cosy Cinema by Roger Thomas.

these were built during the 'cinema mania' following the introduction of talking pictures in 1929. Studley being a big village could justify its own… The Cosy.

There was a covered queuing area, on the wall were posters advertising forthcoming films, and on Saturday afternoons excited youngsters noisily waited for doors to open into a small foyer which housed the ticket office. The cinemagoer then went through heavy red curtains into the auditorium. This was quite splendid, but the shabby carpet and torn seats revealed (in the early 1950s), a building in its initial stages of neglect!

My first memories, just after the war, were of regular Saturday matinees for an admission charge of 6d. Films were in 'black and, white', and included twelve different episodes of Tarzan starring Johnny Weissmuller made between 1932 and 1948. Also popular were Cisco Kid and his Mexican friend Pancho; Roy Rogers and his horse Trigger; as well as other cowboy films starring Hopalong Cassidy. I do not remember any adverts but there was a newsreel and at the end of every performance we stood to sing the Royal Anthem! There was a short interval in most films when the ushers sold ice cream and a tub with wooden spoon was 3d. To round off the afternoon's entertainment we went up to the

Cosy Corner fish and chip shop where a portion of chips and scratchings used up the balance of our 1/- (shilling) per week pocket money.

As I got older, I remember going to see some evening performances and watching colour films like Buffalo Bill and the tales of Uncle Remus. One night I remember, having sobbed the whole way back home, explaining to concerned parents that "Buffalo Bill was gone and wouldn't be coming back!" We also saw lots of black and white war films like 'The Sea shall not have them', 'Gunga Din' and of course 'African Queen'. The price was 1/3d (about 6p) and if you went up in the balcony it was 1/6d. This was about six feet higher than the main auditorium but unlike downstairs it had raked seats on the gently sloping floor. The entrance to the balcony was from outside by a sloping concrete path. Underneath this path were the men's toilets and around the back of the building the ladies' toilets were situated.

In those days, the owner or manager was Terry Thomas look-alike Jack Leuty. He lived in the fine double fronted house in Castle Road, then in its own large grounds which belonged to brewer Jack Thompson. The projectionist was funeral

The interior of the cinema. The image above is a copy of the painting that hung inside the foyer (SLHG).

director Alec Dyer and there would be hoots of laughter and ribald comments when the film broke, as it often did! Ushers Mr Waring or Mrs Tillsley would try in vain to control the audience but there would be loud applause when 'normal service was resumed'!

The only time I ever remember my mother going to the Cosy was with other mothers to assess the suitability of (or was it to enjoy) 'Rock around the Clock'. The newspapers were full of stories of how this film might corrupt young people… there were even stories of kids rocking in the aisles! The nature of cinema had changed and for me it was where I could meet up with my latest girlfriend. These couples sat in the back rows on the right-hand side (looking at the screen) and I swear that Freddy Bennett was in there almost every night! One advantage of meeting your girl in there was that she would pay for her admission, but this went dreadfully wrong for me one night when into the Cosy came my latest flame, her mother, grandmother and little brother… not what I had in mind!

But on a more serious note, this cinema, and our 'Cosy' has been obliterated. Throughout the UK, most cinemas like this one have ceased functioning as such, but the buildings which housed them have been retained and usually provide some cultural use. In Studley this is not the case; only local historians now talk of this centre which was once the cultural and entertainment hub used by people from around this area, as well as the villagers themselves. I could not even find a photograph and so I am doubly appreciative of Roger for bringing the 'Cosy' back to life within his beautiful painting, which reflects its attractiveness to the likes of me. Thank you, Roger.

The Vicarage Hall

There are many things I remember about the Vicarage Hall, especially when part of it was our classroom but the one thing I could not forget, was a picture hanging in the passageway leading to the toilets and beyond that a door leading to the Vicarage. In early 2022 whilst visiting churches in North Norfolk I saw a replica of it and whilst visiting the Vicarage Hall during the SLHG Open Day in 2022, the picture was still there, but within the main hall.

I remember attending wedding receptions and other parties there and if these were on a fine summer's day, we could go into the gardens so beautifully maintained by Mr Lee, the gardener, who was employed by Canon Kemp. Also, the gardens to one side of the lawns were used for gardening classes with teacher

Jack Chambers. Although he might have been criticised for his corporal punishment of a slipper across their backside, there are men in Studley who would readily agree that it was Jack who taught them vital gardening skills.

Together with my mum I have attended Christmas bazaars and rummage sales and, long after we left the village, we would join her there in order to meet up with old friends. Most importantly for me it is where my partner Pat and I attended confirmation classes with Vicar Atcheson.

A copy of Holman Hunt's 'The Light of the World' which hung in the Vicarage Hall at Studley. Photograph by Arthur Cooke.

The Canteen

Situated at one end of Marble Alley before the junction with Alcester Road, the Canteen was more than just a place where workers had their lunches, it was the social centre of Studley, made available for most types of indoor entertainment.

The Canteen in Alcester Road at the Marble Alley junction with the Central Works to the right-hand side. In front of the Canteen is the main bus stop for buses to either Birmingham or Redditch (SLHG).

One of the problems facing local historians, and those wanting to see more of the buildings of the past, is that in those days the majority of people did not own cameras. Unlike in the digital age, the user had to buy film and to have their snapshots developed into photographs, this is why they are so valuable to people like me.

The Canteen was equipped for theatrical performances, as a dance hall, for school events like speech days, as a large meeting hall for local organisations and an assortment of other uses. I remember once going with my mother to see the Studley Operatic Group performing, 'The Pirates of Penzance', and 'HMS Pinafore', and I know there were many more operettas performed. Whilst at my gran's I listened to a local 'Workers' Playtime' broadcast by the BBC and my gran recognised the voices of those employees being interviewed.

On the 'big night out', of Friday, as a dance hall it was most popular with young adults and teenagers, having had their wages and wanting to enjoy themselves. It was very much where 'boy meets girl' and I am sure that it was where one or two permanent partnerships began.

During the week there would be other evening events like this whist drive in the photograph below.

Most importantly for me it was the venue of our wedding reception in September 1962, as I explain later.

A whist drive in the Canteen (SLHG).

High Street

When I was 14 years old, we moved from the Avenue to No. 8 High Street, the house next door to the Co-op butchery which Dad continued to manage until ill health forced him to retire. It is here in the house's shared rear bedroom I lived until the age of 20 when I left the village.

This move to the fourth different house in Studley introduced a completely different world. I was a 'teenager', a word then just invented to describe children which adults, most especially teachers, simply did not understand. We were those born during World War II and we were different from older siblings. This coincided with new recruits, trained during the war, then entering the teaching profession, and only used to a disciplined environment. It helps to explain the problems we had 'growing up'.

The street had changed little since my earlier memories as a child but in 2021 as I drove down it, I found it almost unrecognisable except for important landmarks like the Swan public house. Gone are beautiful cottages now replaced by Albert Close, named after my father, who was, not only a long serving member of Alcester Rural District Council, but also a well-known personality in Studley; so much so, that he always 'topped the poll' at the elections. I recall, the year in which Jack Leuty, manager of the Cosy cinema, or was it Alec Dyer, the projectionist, had a message displayed on the screen for nights before the voting day, saying VOTE FOR ALBERT COOKE! My father, like all the Studley members, was in what they named, the Non-Political Progressive Party, and you can quite imagine the annoyance of their rivals when they learnt of this unauthorised canvassing at the Cosy!

The new development has also replaced some of the old cottages and the wooden doored garage where Jack Swinglehurst stored his Jowett bread delivery van, where the 'missus' kept the confectionery shop next door, the café at the back which we all knew as 'The Singing Kettle' and where the newly created teenagers, like us, had ice-cream sodas whilst listening to the latest rock and roll music on the first juke-box in Studley. The premises next door became the hairdressing salon of Val Mertens, and it was here that my wife-to-be had her hair 'done', in readiness, and not to be in the High Street between certain hours! Further down was the large house of the large Sargeant family with well-known personalities, like their son, Kenny.

Next door to them was a double fronted house with small gardens either side of the path to the front door and here lived the family of Portman, then later of Tustin, following their move from Foster Avenue and later Barry Homer and his family. Next door was Duffin's grocery then, sharing the same porch were two shops, one of which was a hairdresser. Later Duffin's was to become the first DIY shop in the village and was run by Barry Homer.

After the shops was a passageway which we called 'the tuary' which initially led to the side gate of Duffin's and where Mr Duffin kept his large car. One year he took our family to Sandy Bay in Devon, but I do not know whether he did this for others. The tuary also led to the ENTACO playing fields and on the other side to the rear of these dwellings was 'Dysons bank', then further on to the rear of the Wapping, the entrance to the allotments and then to Redditch Road. On the other side of the tuary entrance was the fine terrace of shops, with accommodation above and cottages, which began with Sutor's store. Often seen was Edgar and son John carrying items from there to the shop two doors down. In between Sutor's store and the grocery shop, was the cottage of 'Div' (Elsie) Freeman. Below Sutor's was another cottage and next to it Draycott's grocery.

The house on the end of the terrace was that of Mr and Mrs Crump. At the side of the house was a window and once when Maurice Dyson and I were playing football nearby Mrs Crump understandably moved us on. But the ball went through a window in the Coach and Horses pub and its manager, Mrs Blundell, soon angrily appeared to "sort us out", as she was concerned about a darts competition due that evening. Maurice's Dad, Harold, had been captain of their darts team and was quickly able to pacify her, so I went home!

Coach and Horses Inn, circa 1920 (SLHG).

On the right-hand side of what we called 'Dysons bank' was my great-uncle Harry's cobblers' shop, to the left a large garage, and next to a shop, much smaller then, with the family living at the rear. Then the Coach and Horses, also known as the Central Restaurant.

Next came a cottage where, I believe, a Mr Lamb lived, followed by the house of Mrs Miles and when you entered its front door you were in a flagged floor passageway with rooms on either side. Further on were those cottages whose rear entrances were in the tuary. In the house of Mrs Miles lodged a man named Gordon Fletcher, one of the 'Priory Boys', he and I sometimes cycled to Redditch Swimming Baths.

Co-op Butchery, High Street

Tuesday 24th December 1957
Christmas Eve was always the busiest day of the year for my father as he was the manager of the Alcester Co-operative Society butchers' shop in the High Street. During the preceding weekend dad together with assistant manager Sammy Sutor, Gabby Coles (from Alcester) and I were busy preparing the poultry. There were no frozen products so the turkeys, ducks and chickens that arrived complete with feathers, were plucked, drawn and dressed to be ready for the big day. Sammy was the expert in this art and he could pluck 20 turkeys in the time I would take to do one! I can hear him now, "Don't tear that breast you little b.....!" I was more usefully employed making tea and sweeping up the feathers! This work continued during Monday (normally half-day closing), with the blue window blinds firmly down, as one by one the 'birds' hung in the window. By this time, the refrigerated delivery van parked on the pavement outside as sides of beef, 'Cantos' (New Zealand lamb) and pigs were unloaded, followed by huge strings of sausages, massive pork pies, boxes of sage and onion as well as other stuffing. It needs to be explained that in the meat trade, at that time, the only description given to carcasses of New Zealand lamb, which arrived wrapped in sheep cloth (muslin) was 'Canto', which may have been slang for Canterbury.

The doorway would become congested by those sheltering in there while waiting for the next bus to Redditch. These people had to move to allow the next delivery or customers calling in to place their Christmas orders. Making matters worse was 'Tosker', a big black Labrador that belonged to the Vicar, who spent all day outside the shop. 'Tosker' was joined by 'Tacker' (Sam gave him this name) Biddle, another big black dog, from 'down the Fleece' (Fleece Hill). The next

Alcester Co-operative Wholesale Butchery, High Street, Studley (SLHG).

job was to prepare the rest of the meat as we placed pigs' heads either side of the window shelf and pork pies alongside them. To complete the window display (see above), were rosettes from champion bullocks, tins of corned beef and sprigs of parsley for decoration. Everything was now ready for the big day!

Dad would be there at 5am (we lived next door to the shop) and I started at 7am, by which time the orders for the first round, High Street, Station Road, Node Hill and Crooks Lane were ready for delivery. These were put into the basket of the carrier bike and I was on my way while the orders for later rounds were being made up. By the time I got back the shop was busy with customers collecting their orders and 'tea-time', a half-hourly event! The next delivery was to the Needle Industries canteen in Marble Alley and my cycling skills fully evaluated as I negotiated 'Franklins' Corner with the basket filled with lamb chops. Mrs Vale oversaw the kitchens and was ready to prepare dinner for factory workers. Gabby (David Coles) then did the next deliveries while I took the bloodied boards to the back of the shop, where I scrubbed and washed them. There were also single deliveries that I could make on my own bike which took me as far as Mappleborough or Coughton. Officially there was no credit, all payments were made in cash, but dad sometimes allowed items 'on the slate'. One of my tasks was to visit a certain prefab and I was told what to do, "Knock on the door, then run around to the rear window and you will see Mrs W. trying to hide under the table… tap the window… she will come to the front and offer 2s 6d. Tell her you want 5 shillings", it always worked! I carried a small receipt book and wrote the slip with her 'divi' number and the amount. Every customer had a unique membership number and at the end of the year every payment made was accumulated so as to determine their share of the profits of the Society which were distributed as dividends.

By the afternoon things began to quieten down, everyone became more relaxed and the 'tips' box becoming filled alongside bottles of whisky, sherry and port given by thankful customers. Big white £5, £1 and 10/- notes were taken from the tills, along with my little receipt book which had to be reconciled with my cash bag, and placed in a blue bag which I then took round to the Co-op Grocers opposite the Manor (no Securicor then). Between the grocers and drapers was a raised office in which sat the manager, Tommy Knight. The money was recounted before I left to return to the shop and it was then that the entertainment began!

Factory workers had much to celebrate that year for they would have 3 days off (4 if they normally worked on Saturdays) and the week before was a 'pudding week'. Piece workers (those paid by results, e.g. packs of needles inspected or 'spitted') had an incentive to work much harder to give them a bigger holiday wage packet. Now, having been paid and allowed to leave early, workers began their last-minute shopping: toys, wrapping paper and crackers, from Johnson's 'old Post Office', hardware from Fosters, fish and fruit from Dysons, shoe repairs from Harry Westbury and long queues formed outside Sutor's. During the year workers had been saving a little per week to buy some booze with which to celebrate breaking up for Christmas. The pavements were filled with loud, excited men and women (some it seemed with pleated legs) as they went from shop to shop. Men would squeeze into the shop with their Christmas trees and mistletoe and dad and Sam received quite a few kisses … from the ladies, of course!

Finally, it was time to clean the blocks, the wooden tables, on which the staff cut the meat into various joints. First, we washed these tables with scalding soapy water, then they were scraped with wire brushes and sawdust until clean, the sawdust on the floors was replaced and then our job was done. The tips were distributed between the staff; whisky was added to our teas … we were ready for Christmas!

Rock And Roll And The Singing Kettle

At the same time as Roger's increasing involvement in farming took him further into the countryside, my move to the High Street, at the age of thirteen, took me into becoming a 'townie'. That year, 1955, 'Rock and Roll' was introduced to Britain, with Bill Haley and his Comets' record 'Rock Around the Clock', released into a record market previously dominated by adult listeners. For me and other teenagers two places in Studley made it possible for us to enjoy this music. I did not go to the dances at the Canteen which I talk about later, where no doubt this music influenced their dancing. For me it was the 'Singing Kettle' and The ENTACO Sports Club, both accessible from the High Street.

In the rear of the confectionery and ice cream shop, opposite the Swan PH, and run by the Swinglehurst family, was a café which had the first jukebox in the village. This was my first introduction to this music and amongst the selections were the very latest records.

We teenagers never saw Jack Swinglehurst as he was busy with his bread delivery service but his 'no nonsense missus' kept us in check, provided that we bought at least one ice cream soda, whilst we were there. This drink, in a tall glass with a straw, was simply lemonade with a lump of vanilla ice cream placed in it, and it was lovely. I cannot remember all of those who I might have seen in there, but it would certainly include the gang who, one day went off on a train trip to Rhyl in North Wales, I will write about later. There were similar places for us to go in neighbouring Redditch and Alcester, but this would have involved bus journeys and payment of fares; in any event this book is about Studley.

This was the age of the teddy boy, young men who could afford them, purchased light blue, or perhaps pink, Edwardian suits with 'drainpipe' trousers and thick crepe soled shoes, which we called 'onion treaders'. Now, Arthur Cooke could not afford such a suit so instead it was a long black and white check jacket with light blue star effect drainpipes for me. Bless her, my gran, for whom I could do no wrong, gave my mum her old velvet hat which my mum shaped and sewed on as a collar. Was I smart? I strutted up and down the High Street like I was Elvis Presley himself. To go with this garb was a red shirt with wide opening neckline and patterned with large green stars; I thought I was the bees' knees! A little story which may amuse you concerned an incident when my then girlfriend's father had agreed to pick me up outside Geoff Hill's fish and chip shop en-route to the house of a relative. But he did not. My girlfriend said he could not park as the road was so busy with boys on motorbike. However, I wondered if when he first saw me, he thought it better to drive on?

To purchase a record, would involve a journey into Redditch where there was a shop in which you could enter a booth to listen to them. In those days, there were three variations of laminated records; revolution per minute (rpm), speeds 45, 78, and LP (long play which was 33⅓rpm). By far the most popular was the 78rpm at prices around 6/8d (6 shillings and 8 pence), or 33p in our decimal currency. My first record was Fats Domino's, 'Blueberry Hill' which I played at home until the track was almost worn out.

To do this I needed a record player. Many of us were able to belong to a mail order club and my mum ran one. I should explain that from home she could order items for members who each agreed to pay the same amount. From memory, she had twenty members each paying her 2/6d every week for 40 weeks; a draw would determine the order in which they received their £5 of merchandise, which she would then order. Thus, if you were very lucky, by drawing number 1, you got your items ordered straight away, but if you drew number 20, you waited a long time. I cannot remember how much I had to pay for a portable, mains electric, one disc only play, record player, but this is how I bought mine. Although much better than me playing my record alone was for me to go to the ENTACO Sports Club, which I could easily access from off the 'tuary' opposite to where I lived.

The Entaco Sports Club

I do not know if employees of the Needle Industries had free membership but I had to pay a small annual amount as a junior member. At first my interest there was its snooker hall, where I was never as good as the later legendary player, Steve Davis, but I did perform well against a man from the Wapping, named Davis, whose skill won him the 'Knock-out' trophy each year.

The hall had another attraction for me as, on some evenings, teenagers could stand outside whilst a record player could be plugged into one of the light sockets within the hall. No-one seemed to mind and in fact a player might oblige by taking the plug from us through the open quarter light and plugging it in. My girlfriend, later to be my wife, Pat, had a portable ten-disc record player and when plugged in we were in our 'dance hall'.

Studley Garage And The Spitfire

I know that 'Studleyites' and indeed those who have left the village like me, mourn the loss of so many fine buildings which I have been able to feature in this book. But just a few know what was lost to the village when Studley Garage was demolished.

In his capacity as secretary to the Studley branch of the Royal British Legion dad often had meetings with Graham Hill who was involved with the Legion. On two occasions I had the privilege of climbing the spiral staircase with dad and saw the mural painted walls. Graham's grandson, Graham Hill Jr., explained that "the inside of the tower had a beautiful terrazzo staircase with brass inlays and the tower was painted with a mural depicting all of Graham's interests including various types of aircraft, cars, fields, and wildlife ...".[17]

Referring to the Spitfire aircraft which was placed near the entrance to the Priory and captured in Roger's painting opposite as well as on the rear cover of this book, Graham explained that, "His contacts with the RFC and subsequently the RAF led to the storage of the Spitfire on the forecourt of Studley Garage, which I imagine Studley folk still remember. Despite a huge effort to buy it from the ministry, the RAF turned up with a low loader, cut the wings off with axes and took it away for scrap".

Graham's son Roger explained that after its delivery and reassembly, "It stayed behind the garage with the kind permission of Eric Langston, the superintendent of Priory Farm – it was later moved to the front of the field adjoining the garage, where it stayed for some years".

Co-author of this book, Roger Thomas, believes that the Spitfire did not have an engine and may originally have been destined for Church Green, Redditch but it proved unsuitable for that site. He says that; "the Spitfire, in the 50s, sat in the corner of the Priory Farm field just inside the gateway

Graham Hill (SLHG).

17   *Studley Historian*, Issue 7, pp.9-10 and *SH* Issue 34, pp.4-5, 'The Spitfire & Graham Hill'.

The Spitfire and in the background the Barley Mow by Roger Thomas.

where me and Jimmy Langston, whose father was manager of both Priory Farm and Field Farm, thought we would sit in the Spitfire to try and imagine what it was like to fly it, and there wasn't a lot of room for us. While enjoying ourselves Graham Hill came from the Garage which was next to the field and gave us both a good telling off!"

Blackpool

Quite reasonably you may ask "What has this got to do with Studley?", but many of the 'old-uns' would say "It has a lot to do with Studley and was one of the things we enjoyed the most." It is worth remembering that Studley is a long way from the sea so a weekend in Blackpool for its illuminations was the highlight of many villagers' year. As previously explained only a few people could afford to go away for a summer holiday unless they went to relatives who lived by the sea, but a weekend in Blackpool might be affordable. I first went there with Pat and her family, staying at the Trafalgar Hotel on the seafront, when I was 16 years old and "I got the bug".

Imagine a time, when there were no motorways, the Mersey Tunnel only just thought about and a coach journey from Studley with the driver obliged to cross the notorious Warrington Swing Bridge, where there were often lengthy delays. Workers hurried home to change into their weekend clothes, which included rainwear, hurriedly packed and then off to the pick-up points for the journey. By the time we arrived the lights were switched off, but it did not matter, as we enjoyed the fun and everything which made that place so special. Extremely late on Sunday evening we got home still talking about the fun we'd had.

Hardings coaches awaiting their passengers outside Bill Dyson's house in Foster Avenue (SLHG).

In the photograph above are the sort of coaches we travelled on for our weekend in Blackpool. Judging by the destination blind they appear to be travelling to Weston-super-Mare, possibly on one of the trips that were organised by the local coach companies, or by publicans. I wonder why they were parked in the Avenue? Mrs Harding (née Dyson) from Crabbs Cross was a sister of Bill Dyson, who lived in the Avenue.

Four Elms Farm

Roger worked here and pays tribute to its owner Captain Peart after the postscript at the end of this book.

Studley College

When Roger received a number of back dated issues of SH delivered to his home in Somerset, it prompted him to draft an article which covered many topics; one was Studley Castle, now a hotel, but once the home of a women's agricultural college.

"Seeing Studley College in the Historian reminds me of the times I spent going to the young farmers club, with Bill Palmer as Secretary, in the late 50s early 60s, playing the girls there at table tennis and cricket, jumping out of the way when they sent the cricket ball hurtling down. No wonder I did not take to sport especially when in goal, at the High School, I once let in 18 goals against a Redditch team. This had something to do with Rylma Hopkins, who was standing on the touchline."

When I saw this item included by Roger, it reminded me of "my last bit of mischief" which I told you was planned by Studley Young Conservatives in the committee room of the Studley Conservative Club, in Alcester Road. I need to explain. At the end of every college year was what was known as 'Rag Day' when students would come into the village and do mischievous things, like moving

Studley Castle, circa 1900 (SLHG).

potted shrubs from one place to another. One year they emulsion painted huge footprints from the bridge in Castle Road into the village.

A small group of us, which included Patrick Wainwright, plotted a 'revenge attack' to pre-empt them, by going up to the College in the dead of night. Whilst there we entered the cloakroom where all the girls' yellow, sou'westers, rain hats and wellies were skilfully placed. We rearranged them and I mean rearranged them! Then as we were leaving, we lit a pigeon scarer on the drive, hid in the shadows and when we heard the first loud bang echoing around the castle we ran. My last bit of mischief in Studley.

The War Memorial

In 1946 I stood with my father, who was then secretary to the Studley branch of the Royal British Legion, as you might imagine unaware of what was taking place. There were many men with medals in their lapels, marching bands, army cadets and the nervous bugler, who could only perform whilst standing behind some bushes. This occasion was unlike any other, for it was when the memorial plaque with the names of the Studley victims of the Second World War was unveiled.

The lower part of the war memorial taken on Remembrance Sunday, by courtesy of Studley in Bloom.

My dad would have been enormously proud to see me, on Remembrance Sunday 2019, laying the SLHG wreath on the memorial alongside the others. I remain grateful to them for that opportunity.

Studley And Astwood Bank Station

There are more stories about this railway station appearing in SH than any other and it has special memories for me. My first memories were of travelling, with my mother and elder brother, to and from Broom station, when visiting my Aunty Ida at Bidford-on-Avon. Those journeys were always an adventure, just as the 148 bus journeys were to Evesham and to be able to play in its park. The very last time, shortly before the station closed forever, witnessed me standing on the bridge, whilst waving to Pat, who was travelling to Birmingham to be with her parents for Christmas. I had to stand there, rather than the station platform, as the only member of staff at the station would be travelling on that train.

But the one journey which overshadows them all was a special trip to Rhyl, when on the return journey my romance with Pat Cartmell began, Pat was

Studley and Astwood Bank Station by Roger Thomas.

On the beach at Rhyl, August 1957, photograph taken by Arthur Cooke. Standing left to right, Diane Frogett, Francis Browning, and Roger ('Bandy') Hancox. Sitting left to right, Constance Cartmell, Patricia Cartmell, Marilyn Salmons, Michael Duffin and Frankie Morrall.

sixteen and me, just fifteen. Appearing in the photograph above are some of our gang on what was a busy day on the beach, which of course, has many special memories for me.

My First Car 'PUY 780'

Enzo Ferrari once said; "There is no car like the Mini. The engine turns by pushing a button on the floor".[18] In 1959 the British Motor Corporation, which had absorbed amongst others Austin at Longbridge, Birmingham, launched a revolutionary new car under both Austin and Morris, which was soon to be simply known as the Mini. But did I have one? No! I could not afford one and I could not just go into a bank and ask for a loan, because I was too young. I was a minor of less than twenty-one years of age. However, with my dad guaranteeing the transaction, I did take out a hire purchase agreement in 1961 to buy a second-hand, 1956 registered, Austin A30 which undoubtedly was built in the nearby Longbridge factory. It did not have a push button starter but relied on an

---

18   Cheetham, Craig, *British Cars from 1910*, (2007), pp.28-29.

ignition key inserted near the steering wheel and if that did not work by inserting a starter handle into the crankshaft at the front and vigorously turning it. It was my first car and I still think of it with affection. Especially now in the year 2022 when there is much talk of the cost of filling the tank of a family car being £100. The petrol I used was named Power and cost 4/8d (four shillings and eight pence) and I received change from a £1 note after filling the tank! Also, the method of filling of tanks had improved, for although it still had to be done by an attendant, most pumps were electrically powered.

St Mary's Parish Church, Studley And Two Vicars

The church played such a vital role in our lives, there were three vicars during my years at Studley, the first was the Reverend Banting who christened me there although I was too young to remember.

But I vividly remember my first experience of Canon Kemp. It was after having fallen into the paddling pool at Warwick, having newspaper stuffed up my soaking trouser legs and shirt, being carried by him to the awaiting coach. This was the Sunday school annual outing, often taking us to Warwick to visit the castle and then for a picnic in the surrounding park. We always found time to go into Woolworths and buy small plastic boats which we sailed down an

St Mary's Parish Church (photograph courtesy Alistair Brewin).

Pam Draycott presenting flowers to Lady Mills, from the Manor, being watched by Canon Kemp, who was standing behind her. In the centre is Mr Cullum's wife. Pam Draycott (SLHG).

ornamental stream in the park. Years later my wife and I revisited the Park and were upset to see the overgrown and barely visible stream, but the pool was still there. We watched as an unfortunate child fell in, just as I must have done all those years before. But this child had a change of clothes! Mrs Kemp was also a very loving and warm person, and it seemed to me, that in their very different roles, they were the softer face of both the church and the C. of E. School.

My family, although not regular churchgoers, were keen supporters of the various church activities, so we saw the vicar quite a lot. Canon Kemp, was also the chair of the 'Big School' (C. of E. School) governors, so we often saw him there. The gardener at the Vicarage was a Mr Lee, who I think lived in Crooks Lane. He was a jolly man and I believe shared home-grown tobacco with the vicar and Mr ('Spud') Taylor, headmaster of the school. These leaves grew in a glass frame situated between the vicarage and the hall, and to me, as a child, the gardens were massive and well maintained.

When Canon and Mrs Kemp left Studley for the village of Brailes, he was replaced by the Reverend Atcheson, who was a very different sort of vicar. I know

The Reverend Atcheson at the wedding of Tony and Jean (née Crook) Lever (photograph courtesy Tony Lever).

nothing of the comparative wealth of the two men, or of the Church's finances, but the grounds of the vicarage quickly deteriorated, I assume, for lack of funds. But the new vicar was to play a most important part in the lives of my wife Pat and myself.

You may recall in my introduction, it was my godparents, aunty Elsie and uncle Gerald Read, who took me to the church for my christening. They took the vows they had made very seriously and my aunt asked several times when I would be confirmed. I did not disappoint them, because, together with Pat, we were confirmed at the same time, after attending confirmation lessons with the vicar, which were held both in the Vicarage Hall and the Vicarage itself. We had been regular attendees, so much so, that the vicar said, that it was as if we had already been joined together.

The event was not without both worrying and funny moments. To begin with I forgot to order a bridal car and thank goodness, Hill's Garage came to the rescue, in picking up Pat and the bridesmaids then taking them to the church. I drove the best man, my brother, Peter there in advance of that. Then the vicar forgot to bring the church register with him so a cousin was asked to go to the vicarage to collect it, finally the photographers did not turn up until after the service! When we were in the vestry afterwards Reverend Atcheson realised that I was too young to marry without the consent of my parents, as in 1962, the age for adults was 21 years! But in his characteristic style he asked both of my parents to sign the register, as he said to them, "now I know that you both agree!" When we came out of the church the photo session was shortened as there was another marriage service immediately afterwards.

Patricia and Arthur Cooke on 1st September 1962 (Arthur Cooke Collection).

Not that any of these things spoilt the day, as we were taken to our DIY reception, provided by dad, at the Canteen, of course. Manageress, Mrs Vale did all of the sandwiches, trifles and jellies but no doubt these were supplemented by provisions brought by relatives. Uncle Lionel ran the free bar, Pat's aunt Edna was the MC, and Jack Treadgold, from Alcester Road, entertained us with his piano accordion.

We had our first night in the bed of my mum and dad, but practical jokers had already made it into an 'apple pie' bed into which we could not get our legs and the po had fizzy health salts put inside so I will leave the rest of this story to your imagination.

Early the following morning we left Studley in our Austin A30 car. We were never again, to reside in the village we both loved.

This is the end of my story and of this book. Except for the postscript.

Patricia and Arthur Cooke's Austin A30 car, PUY 780 (Arthur Cooke Collection).

POSTSCRIPT

WHENEVER I write a letter, I inevitably add a PS, so why not in this book? Likewise, after mine, Roger will do the same.

You might imagine that, having married and left the village, my links with John would end, especially as most people had no house phone, yet alone mobile phone and no-one had heard of the internet. But fortunately, John, like my sister-in-law Con and husband, Howard Vale were 'Blues' fans, i.e. they supported Birmingham City Football Club. Furthermore, they all had stadium seats near to one another. The Vales arranged a reunion between Pat and me and John and his wife, Rhona, and despite the distance between us, our friendship rekindled. Sadly, the premature death of Rhona occurred, and it was a while before we could meet again for two nostalgic walks.

On two occasions I travelled to Studley, staying overnight at my parents' bungalow, 'Shangri-la', off Station Road. Early the next day, John's son, Kevin, dropped his dad off in readiness for early walks. As the contents of this book are limited to the period, 1941-1962, I am sure you will not mind if I tell you about them, and of my tribute to John.

The first walk took us up Station Road, then turning left and just over the brow of the hill we crossed to take a track to a spinney, where we once saw an owl in the treetops, but not on this occasion. We headed in the direction of Sambourne travelled along what remained of the old railway line to a spinney, which was opposite, the now redundant, Coughton Station. We had to divert several times as we were faced with notices telling us the property was 'PRIVATE'. We were grown-ups by then so we were not naughty, but we did once, finish in someone's garden. The pampas grass was still there just as before and we may have jumped up and down and pretended to be lost, but then moving on. We knew the line of the small stream and spring and arrived at the point where the stream from Broadmarsh flows into Middletown Brook. No, we did not build dams, as we did not have the time, but we did drink cool fresh water from the spring as we remembered those times together.

We continued downstream and crossed the road at Coughton, then alongside Coughton Court but then, I think, we cheated a bit and crossed the river where we ought not to have done, finally upstream towards Spernall. John's fascination with the redundant church there became so apparent and he told me it was here that he would like 'to be laid to rest'. We crossed the road and went upstream alongside Cleeton's Farm where we talked about the role Mrs Cleeton had played while we were at Infant School, inviting our class to see the operation of its dairy.

We continued past the farm upstream towards the Park and I was amazed by the changes in the watercourse, effected by river engineers to reduce the risks of flooding, the likes of which we had witnessed many times before. From my recollections of that walk, we did not take water or food; we just talked. We went into the Barley Mow for food, then later on son, Kevin, joined us and we kept talking between ourselves. Sometime later a server tapped my shoulder, to tell me that the pub had closed, and we were completely oblivious to the time, but it was a super day.

The next walk was to give us a lovely surprise for as we walked past the house of John and Sybil Watton in Crooks Lane, we saw that John was at the top of a ladder and shouted up to him. He was as surprised as we were and rapidly came down the ladder, 'fire-officer style', with feet not touching the rungs. We went for coffee and a chat as well as the obligatory tour of John's shed with its amazing collection of tools. 'For two pins', John would have joined us, but he had work to do and so we carried on towards Middletown Brook, down the 'ills and 'ollers and around an area which was changed in parts but still giving us plenty to talk about.

Walking along downstream on its right bank towards Sambourne Lane was not as easy as it was many years before, but we managed and then doubled back to Middletown taking a track over to where we last saw Howell's barn and then across in the direction of Sadler's Wood, then upstream to Broadmarsh and along the road towards the redundant Studley and Sambourne station. We called in to see my parents and then off to the Barley Mow again, still talking, but intent on not over-staying our welcome this time.

Here in Essex in 1990 I joined the Ramblers Association and for more than twenty years I led walks for separate groups. I was once privileged to perform the eulogy at the funeral of our chairperson, who like John, had died of dementia. I recalled that the part I liked the most about the walks he led, was the appreciation of the walkers. So, at the end of my contribution, I went to the coffin to say, "thank you, for your final walk, it was very good". Now in closing this section of my book I pay tribute to John and all the fantastic adventures, the knowledge of the countryside, the mischief, the reunion, and then much later the happy days in the company of John and his partner, Karen. Thank you, John.

I last saw John in a nursing home in Droitwich, together with Karen, when we visited him. It seems appropriate now, as it was Remembrance Sunday and earlier that day I laid the SLHG wreath on the war memorial. Sadly, but inevitably, he died in 2020 and because of lock-down restrictions at that time, I could not be at the funeral service. Ironically, the following year, in 2021, my wife passed away and similar circumstances applied, with Karen only able to watch a video of the service in the same way as Pat and I viewed John's funeral.

In thinking of John, I also pay tribute to Karen for so many things. Not just the way that she supported him, through his deteriorating health, but increasingly supporting his editorship of the SH; in such a way that only the officers of SLHG would know that she was doing the work. During this time, she also played an increasingly active role as a committee member of SLHG. Karen also played a big part in the production of my last book about the War Memorial. The same applies with this book, as without her help, to Roger and me, it might never have been completed. My thanks also go to Arthur Daniels, for his continuing support and to Tony Lever, for finding those photographs for the book which had eluded me.

But look, this is a happy book, about happy things and I will end with a funny, at least I hope you will think it funny?

In 1989 I 'retired', aged forty-nine from the lofty heights of my Council chief executive position. The politics of the council had changed, I had been CE for 10 years, and the new administration thought I was unable to adjust to them. The Council thought I had served them well, even the new lot, and they would run the elections of 1991 as well as some other things. I could have 'gardening leave' until after my 50th birthday. Those were the days. As a teenager, like so many others, my parents could not afford for me to go to university and this was a unique chance of putting that right. I had earlier been studying for an 'A' level in history at night school and my tutor supported my application for a BA place at the University of Essex. I did not drive there in my Council car which I could keep for a while but instead by train and coach just like the other potential undergraduates. I'm sure that they all thought I must be a dad or a grandad! But when it came to my interview with a professor, the Head of the History Department, at first it did not look good. In a scene that could have been taken from the film, *Educating Rita*, he seemed reluctant to accept me. After a while, and here comes the funny bit, he said quite sternly, "OK but shall we say a grade in your 'A' level?" to which I replied, "I think that's unfair, all of these youngsters around me are at school and that might be fair for them, but I'm at work and having to do evening council meetings as well". He looked even more puzzled, so I continued, "And what's more with the tax I have been paying I've earned this place." He sat back on his chair and laughed, whilst saying, "Never in all of my years interviewing young people has anyone said that to me, I'm giving you an unconditional offer, and will rely on your tutor's letter". I was not to disappoint him as on the day of my graduation I reminded him of that, when collecting my certificate of a 2.1. Two years later I was back there for my Master's and during that period I was also awarded a PGCE by the Open University. So, in my life, my adventurism and my sense of humour continues, as it does with Roger, as you will hear in his postscript story about Anne Hathaway's cottage.

Arthur

Anne Hathaway's cottage at Stratford-on-Avon

While visiting Stratford-on-Avon and again Anne Hathaway's cottage, my wife and I decided to go to the café opposite the Cottage. While there the manageress

Anne Hathaway's cottage at Stratford-on-Avon by Roger Thomas.

asked me if we had visited before. Wow, what memories came flooding back and I thought I must tell her.

64 years ago, being 15 years old, I sat in the corner of the café garden painting Anne Hathaway's cottage in oils, having cycled 12 miles from Studley with all my equipment.

While finishing the painting, 'Lupines in all Colours', an American lady asked me if I wanted to sell it. I replied yes, said I was poor and didn't have much money, then agreed a price of £6.00. The lady picked up the painting and plonked it in her bag, it was a good job I had painted about 95 percent of it a few weeks before, only the lupines were still wet. I think I whistled all the way home to Studley. The manageress laughed and said "what a lovely story, have the drinks on me". She wouldn't take any money.

Roger

REFERENCES

THE FOLLOWING are references to the *Studley Historian* with the issue and page numbers in which the articles appeared:

Studley Historian, Issue 10, pp.4-6, 'The Blicks of Studley'.
Studley Historian, Issue 11, pp.4-7, 'The Cookes of Studley'.
Studley Historian, Issue 16, p.9 and *SH* Issue 24, pp.3-6, 'The Wattons of Studley'.
Studley Historian, Issue 28, pp.16-19, 'Node Hill – On the Edge'.
Studley Historian, Issue 27, pp.14-15, 'Hills and Hollows'.
Studley Historian, Issue 34, pp.11-12, 'Studley Mop in the 1950s'.
Studley Historian, Issue 20, pp.3-4, 'Needle Inspection'.
Studley Historian, Issue 32, pp.11-12, 'Studley Fire Brigade'.
Studley Historian, Issue 19, pp.5-7, 'Studley Telephone Exchange'.
Studley Historian, Issue 7, pp.9-10 and *SH* Issue 34, pp.4-5, 'The Spitfire & Graham Hill'.

The following references are to publications where quotations have been used:
Page 1, Hyams, Jacky, *The Day the War Ended*, (2020).
Pages 28-29, Cheetham, Craig, *British Cars from 1910*, (2007).

Extracts from the following poems have been used:
Jones, Thomas Jr., *Sometimes*.
Wordsworth, William, *I wondered lonely as a cloud*.

Other references to film and literature:
Nesbit, Edith. *The Railway Children*.
Uncle Remus, a fictional character who narrated tales about Afro-Americans.
Educating Rita, 1983, film starring Julie Walters & Michael Caine.

RECOMMENDED READING

Studley Through Time (2016), Alistair Brewin, Brewin Books.

Studley War Memorial Centenary (2020), Arthur Cooke.

Needle Making in Studley (2017), Arthur Cooke.

Studley Historian 46. 12-14. Contains a list of the articles in SH regarding the railway station.

Studley Historian 31. 7-9; 32. 8-10; & 33 12-14. 'Childhood Memories of the Fifties and Early Sixties' (of Studley) by Valma Cooper (née Smith).

Appendix 1

REFLECTIONS

TWO BOYS in the village of Studley, during war-time Britain, whose fathers were away from home serving in the armed services, shared another thing in common, their love of the countryside.

At a time when it seemed to them it was quite safe to wander off, they did not have far to go to enter, 'another world'.

As they grew older, they became even more adventurous, whilst on their own or in the company of others. They listened to the fascinating stories of an older generation and were influenced by them. Whilst at school, they faced disciplinary action by teachers, which today would be illegal, but it did not suppress their mischievousness.

These boys were of a new generation, one which their elders did not understand and so gave them a new name, that of teenagers. At an early age they both did part-time work for the pocket money, with which they could buy the means of expressing themselves. One of them with pens and pencils to write words and the other one in paint to create the pictures embedded in their minds, of 'another world', on the edge of the village.

Coincidentally, as young men they left Studley, one to the Southeast and one to the Southwest, never to reside there again, but their love of the village never left them, as they began to express themselves in articles within the *Studley Historian*.

Now more than seventy years later they are together in this book to share their adventures with those who also have cherished memories of Studley.

We are those two men who are still boys at heart and the picture which most comes to mind is, like those words of the immortal poet Wordsworth, when he describes what he saw, in one of the nation's favourite poems, 'I wondered lonely as a cloud', in these words:

"…they flash upon the inward eye which is the bliss of solitude. And then my heart with pleasure fills and dances with the daffodils."

The bridge to another world by Roger Thomas.

Our inward eye reveals this one, the bridge to 'another world'.

It has been difficult for us to choose both the title of this book and the format for the covers, as the latter should show immediately identifiable places in the village. However, the front cover is something quite different, as the stile, with the field and woods beyond are saying to you, "Climb this stile and then come and join us in our adventures."

Appendix 2

JOHN SHAKLES 1941-2020
By Karen Cording

I CAST my mind back to 1985 when I was single and living in Portsmouth. My mum telephoned me at work one day to say that Guy Mitchell (her favourite artist) was touring in the UK and happened to be appearing at Ferneham Hall, Fareham and would I like to go with her to see him? Yes of course I would. We duly attended the concert and joined the Guy Mitchell Appreciation Society on the spot. The following year Guy was in the UK once again, this time the promoter was Peter G Foot. Long story short we went to another Guy concert where I met Peter. Later that year Peter and I became a couple and in 1987 I toured the UK with Peter doing 13 Guy

John Shakles.

Mitchell concerts in 17 days. What has all this got to do with John Shakles I hear you ask? Well, in addition to promoting and producing shows Peter also managed various artists including Edmund Hockridge, Moira Anderson, Bobby Crush to name but a few. Over the coming few years I was at many Edmund Hockridge concerts with Peter and/or my mum in various parts of the UK; including the Palace Theatre, Redditch on 24th October 1992. (Peter and I parted as a couple in 1991 but have remained very good friends even to this day).

The Palace Theatre, Redditch is where mum (Kathy) and I first met John & Rhona who were also attending the show! After some persuasion by Kathy, who was chairman, John joined the Edmund Hockridge Appreciation Society after the show. EHAS held their AGM at the Norfolk Hotel in Edgbaston in March 1993; John attended and spent the afternoon of the meeting sat with me and mum. A couple of years later Edmund was again appearing at the Palace Theatre, we travelled from Portsmouth, and were staying at the Southcrest Hotel ready for the show in the evening. John and Rhona invited us to lunch at their home in Hillmorton Close and we all met up again in the evening.

During the intervening years the four of us remained friends exchanging letters, Christmas cards and phone calls. Fast forward many years; Kathy died in 2000 and Rhona in 2001. I invited John to attend the EHAS AGM at Leamington in 2002 and 2003 but he was unable to attend as he was a season ticket holder at Birmingham City FC and they were playing at home! However, on 27th March 2004, despite the Blues being at home to Leeds United, John came to the AGM in Leamington; romance blossomed, a few weeks later John came to visit me in Portsmouth for a weekend and most weekends after that. I visited him in Redditch a few times during that summer in between his visits to Portsmouth. As time went by this was so much more than a fleeting romance. Many long discussions were had about a future together. By December 2004 John had retired early from his job as a haberdashery sales representative, I had resigned from my one and only job of 27 years, put my house on the market and left all my family to move to Redditch on Christmas Eve 2004.

The rest as they say is history.

Kathy, John and Karen.

Edmund Hockridge and John.

After John died I was sorting through the mound of 'stuff' in his office and came across a journal of his life which he had been writing for his sons, Kevin and Gary. He started writing this way back in 1974 although the memories were from much earlier before he met his wife at the end of the 1950s.

His entries from March & May 2004 made such lovely reading!

"Saturday March 27th 2004 (written two days later) went to Leamington Spa and met up with Karen Cording again. She looked stunning. I don't know what happened but I couldn't get her out of my mind. A spark had ignited in my brain, all my thoughts are of her and two days on I still feel the same. I'm trying to pluck up the courage to visit her in Portsmouth. I know I'm nearly old enough to be her dad, but she says she likes older men!

Wednesday May 12th 2004. Rang Karen and said I'm coming down this weekend. I'm a complete bag of nerves as I don't know what to expect. What I do know is that I've got to see her – if I don't I know I shall regret it!

*Monday May 17th 2004. I came back home last night – emotions all over the place. I've fallen in love with her. I don't know what I am going to do. I don't know how you two boys will take it but I want to spend the rest of my life with her. It will be a big step for both of us but I **know** that it **will** happen. Don't know when, don't know where, but it **will**!"*

Appendix 3

CAPTAIN PEART 1885-1963
By Roger Thomas

CAPTAIN JOSEPH Peart was a Derbyshire man who owned both Middletown and Four Elms Farms, bordering Studley station and the railway line. The fields included the Hills and Hollows, the old Hollow Oak Tree and the brook, where I spent many happy hours in the 50s and 60s.

We played football in the field opposite my house in Middletown Lane using jackets for goal posts. At the gate stood Captain Peart watching us play; he did not object to us using the field. He was a short stocky man with a moustache, wearing a trilby and had arrived in his green Rover 90. He was like Capt. Mainwaring from Dad's Army!

Later on, I knew Captain Peart quite well as I worked on both the farms before and after leaving school, working in the fields I had played in as a young lad.

I soon found out Captain Peart was a very good portrait and landscape painter, having exhibited in the Derby Art Gallery on many occasions. This was perfect for me, as when I mentioned that I also painted in oils he took a real interest in me, giving me the opportunity to comment on his portraits in progress. He took me to paint bluebells up the Lickey Hills and gave me the inspiration to carry on painting. I still have some of the oil paints and brushes he gave me.

Captain Peart also kept bees and made very good honey. On his trips to the bakery and confectionery shop he owned in Allenton, Derby, he brought back large bags of sugar to feed the bees in winter.

The honey was excellent, as was a half-bottle of rum I remember him giving me when I went down with a very heavy flu-like cold. He said to heat the rum in a saucepan and add half the jar of honey. He didn't say only half the rum… What a hangover I had the next day but I still turned up for milking at 6am in the morning!

That winter, 1960, was particularly cold and Mrs Peart handed me Capt. Peart's spare long johns which she had patched. Being the short man that he was, they fitted me.

I have recently researched Captain J.B. Peart's connection with a famous Derbyshire artist, who helped to save the Rolls Royce factory in the second World War, but we will save that for another time...

Appendix 4

OLD STUDLEY DIALECT

(As spoken by our gran and some others)

Old Studley	English dictionary
appnd	happened
bin	been
babby	baby
bout	about
Brum	Birmingham
cos	because
cud	could
cum	come
doont	don't
e	he
ent	isn't or aren't
er	her
ere	here or ear
gud	good
nuf	enough
nowt	nothing
sed	said
spose	suppose
sprise	surprise
sumit or sumuth	something
ull	will
um	home
wot(s)	what(s)

Readers who are interested in a fuller vocabulary are invited to read Arthur Newbould's *Worcestershire Wise*, ISBN 0953605612.

Appendix 5

STUDLEY PARISH LANDS CHARITIES

By Arthur Daniels

THE WHOLE of the net proceeds of this publication will be donated to the Studley Lands Charities (reg. 214165A).

The Studley Parish Lands Charities comprises seventeen individual bequests of land charges, the earliest of them being recorded in 1658.

The charities' aim was to provide help to those in need; that is the poor who resided within the parish boundary. One of the bequests decreed that half-a-crown shall be given annually to the minister for preaching a sermon twice yearly.

Nearer our own time, have been bequests for the education of children, tea, sugar and gowns to poor widows (no mention of poor men!).

Today, the bread doles, gowns, linen tickets and the vicar's half-crown are gone, to be replaced by their modern counterparts. The income derived from investments enables financial help to be given to individuals in times of crisis; grants to hospitals and schools; homes for the elderly; the education of young people and religious projects.

The generosity of those early benefactors, such as Hobbins, James, Court Dewes and Thomas Chambers lives on. One rent-charge remains, a reminder to the current trustees of the mantle they inherited and which they continue to discretely discharge.